Focus Master:

37 Tips to Stay Present, Ignore Distractions, and Finish the Task at Hand

by Nick Trenton

www.NickTrenton.com

Table of Contents

Chapter 1: Why You're a Couch Potato

"Procrastination is opportunity's assassin."
- Victor Kiam

You have met procrastination before. It needs no introduction, especially when you've known it all your life. Since the moment you were old enough to recognize that you actually have the option to build a Lego castle rather than sit down to do your math homework, procrastination has been there in the background as the devil on your shoulder, encouraging you to do what is worst for you. It's like your shadow; you just can't shake it, it's always with you, and it's easy to forget about.

But unlike your shadow, it's dead set on ruining your life!

Now you're stuck with it and are having problems because it's starting to control you, like one of those relationships that started out fun and exciting but gradually morphed into something that just caused you unhappiness. *You know the ones I'm talking about.* So you want to break up with it to get your life back on track, but you don't know how.

The answer in finally regaining control from the demoralizing domination of procrastination starts with understanding what you are dealing with and how you continually get tricked into handing over the reins to it over and over again.

The term "procrastination" was derived from the Latin *pro*, meaning "forward, forth, or in favor of," and *crastinus*, meaning "of tomorrow." Its literal translation can thus be taken to be the moving forward of something to tomorrow or favoring tomorrow as the ideal time. Action is never for today; it's always another moment to be dealt with later.

For our purposes, procrastination is the act or habit of putting off something to a future time. It involves delaying what needs to be done until the last moment, often to the endpoint of not doing it at all. It involves a certain amount of self-sabotage and ignorance of any future consequences. It causes undue stress and anxiety, often at the pursuit of short-term gratification. It is responsible for an untold number of lost opportunities.

However, it's a mistake to assume that procrastination occurs simply because there is boredom or discomfort. They are parts of the problem, but in reality, much more goes into our lack of action. Just tackling an alleged lack of motivation and interest in something you need to do only shallowly addresses procrastination.

For instance, the thought of having to write out a twenty-thousand-word research paper will certainly cause feelings of boredom and discomfort, so you may delay working on the task for as long as you can. A movie sounds more fun, stimulating, and comfortable.

The next thing you know, you've put off writing the paper until it's just a day before the deadline—which wasn't exactly a rational move, given the sheer size of work involved. You feel guilt and shame about letting things get that far, but you still didn't sit at your computer to start typing. You miss your deadline, lose your job, and your cat runs away from home.

Suppose the twenty-thousand-word research paper was on a topic that you found stimulating and fun and comfortable. Are you so sure that you would wake up eagerly each morning, ready to start typing and editing? It might help, but it's still an unpleasant activity that you would rather substitute with fun. Also, consider how many things you currently avoid even though they are relatively fun and comfortable. They are too numerous to name. This means there is something deeper going on here that keeps you glued to your couch, physically or figuratively. In fact, there is a cycle that researchers have articulated, and this is the first of the reasons in this chapter that you are a couch potato.

The Procrastination Cycle

Let me tell you a story. If you're reading this book, however, it's probably a story that you're sadly all too familiar with. You have the Big Thing to do. You have three days to do it. No big deal, you think, you've easily done things like it before, and you can do it again. Day one, you put it off. No problem, you can do it in three days. Day two, you stare at the unfinished Big Thing and feel vaguely resentful, telling yourself that you have plenty of time and can do it later. Besides, life's for living and it's a beautiful day outside.

Day three rolls around and suddenly the Big Thing is due for the following day. All at once, you feel a little sick about the whole thing. It keeps popping up in your mind, and you can't relax. There seems to be a growing forcefield around the Big Thing. Slowly, it starts to seem much harder to finish than it did just a few days ago . . .

You're feeling really bad now and hating yourself with each passing minute that you don't start. But you continue to push it off, "relaxing" with something you think you want to do instead, but all the time stressing about the work you're not doing. Eventually, at the eleventh hour, you finish the Big Thing at last, but you rush the job and barely scrape by.

Congratulations. You've gone one full cycle on the maddening and super-sabotaging procrastination loop!

Procrastination isn't a personality trait, a bad habit, or an unavoidable fact of life, though. It's a learned pattern of behavior that is cyclical and fully reversible—if you understand how it works.

In some ways, the existence of a *cycle* is a relief because it means that beating procrastination isn't so much about reaching deep inside yourself and relying on your guts to get the job done (although sometimes that part cannot be avoided). It's actually about understanding the cycle of laziness and disrupting it before you get sucked into it.

It's the equivalent of understanding how to use a certain physics equation to solve a problem versus trying to solve the problem differently each time and sometimes just trying out twenty different possibilities. When you know what you're looking for, you're just going to be far more effective. In practical terms, this means that doing what you need to do will be much less of a struggle in the end.

There are five main phases of the cycle that explain why you tend to keep sitting on your butt even though you know you shouldn't be. It further explains how you justify sitting on your butt and even how you'll probably sit on your butt even more decisively the next time. We can follow along with an example of washing a car. You'll soon see how simplistic attributing procrastination to boredom or laziness is.

1. **Unhelpful assumptions or made-up rules**: "Life is short, so I should enjoy it and not spend my precious time washing that dusty car! Car washes are something you pay for, anyway!"
2. **Increasing discomfort**: "I'd rather not wash the car. It's boring and uncomfortable. I know my spouse asked me to, but it can wait."
3. **Excuses for procrastination to decrease psychological discomfort**: "It's perfectly reasonable for me not to wash the car. It's

so hot outside, I would melt. My spouse didn't really mean it when they asked."

4. **Avoidance activities to decrease psychological discomfort**: "I will clean the bathroom instead. I'm still productive! I'll also arrange my desk. Lots of things getting done today. I did pretty well today, all things considered."

5. **Negative and positive consequences**: "Ah, I feel better about myself now. Cleanliness all around. Oh, wait. I still need to wash that car, and my spouse seems angrier this time . . ."

Which brings us full circle: the car isn't washed, and your assumptions remain the same if not reinforced, only this time, there's even more discomfort that you want to avoid immediately. And so it goes on. Once you're in the cycle, it's hard to get over the increasing inertia keeping you from getting the task done.

Let's take a look at each of the phases individually. We'll start right from the top; this is where you are either failing to start a task or to complete a task already underway. You know you should do these things and they are in your best interests. However, you've already made the decision against self-discipline, so what goes through your mind?

Unhelpful Assumptions or Made-Up Rules

If you feel like you don't want to start or follow through with something, it's not due to simple laziness or "I don't feel like it right now." It's about the beliefs and assumptions that underlie these feelings. What are some of these unhelpful assumptions or made-up rules?

My life should be about seeking pleasure, having fun, and enjoying myself. Anything that conflicts with that shouldn't be allowed. We all fall into this at one time or another. Pleasure-seeking is where you feel that life is too short to pass up something fun, interesting, or pleasant in favor of things that may seem boring or hard. Fun is the priority! At the very least, you believe that the current short-term pleasure is more important than a long-term payoff.

This is the true meaning of "I don't feel like it right now"—you are actually saying, "I want to do something more pleasurable than that right now."

I need X, Y, or Z to get to work, and if they are not present, I am excused. Sometimes you just can't muster up the energy to do something. You may feel tired, stressed, depressed, or unmotivated and use that as your "reason" for not getting things done. You have to be "ready." You need X, Y, and Z to start properly. You have to be *in the mood*. All these so-called requirements were conjured by you; none of them actually reflect reality.

I probably won't do it right, so I just won't do it at all. You may fall into the assumption that you must do things perfectly every time or else it will be labeled a failure. This is a fear of failure and rejection, and it also involves a lack of self-confidence. You also don't want others to think less of you. And how do you ensure that neither of these things happen? You don't do it. You don't start it, and you don't finish it. There won't be failure or disappointment because you don't allow the opportunity for judgment.

If you feel that you need to do something that goes against your beliefs, you will only do it when absolutely necessary. This is a reality of human behavior, as is the fact that these beliefs are usually subconscious. So what happens if you are told to do household chores but you possess the first two beliefs of "fun comes first" and "I need perfect conditions"? You'll have fun first and then wait for a large set of preconditions, and the chores will go undone. The *rest* of the cycle is what *keeps* them undone.

Quickly recall a moment in your own past when you were trapped in the procrastination cycle. It might be tricky to identify, but can you see any hints of the underlying beliefs or "rules" you had that instigated the start of your avoidance behavior? This is a rich vein to tap, and once you start looking, you may be surprised by your own hidden assumptions and biases, for example:

"Work shouldn't ever be uncomfortable or boring."

"I can't work on something unless I'm feeling one hundred percent inspired."

"If I dawdle, someone else might step up and do it for me."

"If I don't do this thing I secretly resent, the task may be taken away from me and I'll be relieved of it without having to outright say I don't actually want to do it."

And so on . . .

Increasing Discomfort

When you are procrastinating, you're not totally unaware of what you need to do, and thus tension and discomfort will be created. Knowing you are being naughty does not promote good feelings.

You will have a range of emotions, all of which are uncomfortable: anger, boredom, frustration, exhaustion, resentment, anxiety, embarrassment, fear, or despair. The end result is that we are in an agitated state, and *we don't like feeling this way.* Something will need to change. Think of it this way: your brain doesn't want you to stay in a state of psychological discomfort—it's like standing on the bow of a sinking ship—so it deals with it the only way it knows how: through the next two phases.

(Additionally, if the source of this discomfort is anything having to do with washing that darned car, that means you're going to avoid it like the black plague.)

Making Excuses

Excuses are the first way to make yourself feel better when you are ducking responsibility. They're how you attempt to squash that rising discomfort. You know you should do something, but you don't want to. Does this mean you're just lazy, tired, or entitled to no action? *Of course not.*

Admitting those would cause even more discomfort and tension than you already feel. So you construct excuses to remain the good guy or even victim in your situation—or at least not the bad guy. Now that's a comforting thought. What would you say to make your lack of action acceptable?

"I don't want to miss out on that party tonight. I'll do it tomorrow."

"I'm just too tired tonight. I'll start working on that goal later."

"I'll do a better job on that project when I'm in the mood to work on it."

"I don't have everything I need to finish the job, so I can't start now."

"I'll do it right after I finish this other task."

Now, if you uttered these to someone else, they might reply with a raised eyebrow and a, "Really . . .?" The problem is, these excuses are ones that you tell yourself. And you've probably used them so frequently in your life that the lines between your excuses and reality have blurred. You become unable to discern or tell the truth, and you unknowingly start to disempower yourself.

Somewhere deep in the back of your mind, you *know* that these are excuses. And this means you know they're bogus, and so the tension never really disappears—not for long, anyway. So you might tell yourself, "I won't do it. I'm exhausted. I deserve a long break tonight," and you sit down with a Netflix show and a bag of chips, but you're never genuinely relaxing because the tension is lurking just out of conscious awareness, and you only have a flimsy excuse to ward it off!

And while you're busy convincing yourself that these excuses are real and legitimate, you are smoothly transitioning into the next phase in the cycle: avoidance activities.

Avoidance Activities

Avoidance activities are the culmination of alleviating your discomfort and wanting to feel like you aren't simply being lazy. The internal dialogue goes something like this: "I'm sufficiently justified in not washing the car, but why do I still feel lousy about myself? I should *do* something . . ." Excuses on their own may not be enough, so you figure some action is still needed to lessen the discomfort and tension.

And so you act, though it's never what you should be doing in the first place. Typically, there are two types of avoidance activities. First, there are activities that simply distract you from the discomfort of choosing not to exercise your self-discipline or violate a belief or assumption. Out of sight, out of mind, and the discomfort is destroyed by going for ice cream or to a new superhero movie. This is distraction to the point of denial.

Second, there are activities that make you feel productive in some other way than the task at hand. For instance, if you work from home and are putting off a project, you will never have a cleaner bathroom than when real tasks are to be avoided. You might do an "easier" or lower-priority task. These avoidance activities allow you to say, "Well, at least I did something and wasn't totally unproductive with my time!" A fitting term for these activities is *productive procrastination.*

These activities do help you feel better about yourself in the short term, but they don't move you any closer to where you should be and make the cycle harder to break.

Negative and Positive Consequences

Avoiding is an art. But when you avoid responsibilities, there are always consequences. Somewhere, something is slipping through the cracks. The negative consequences are more obvious. They can include increased discomfort, guilt, anxiety, and shame. You know you're not achieving (or taking steps to achieve) your goal, and this just makes you feel worse.

Another negative consequence is having increased demands on you. Your work may accumulate, leaving you to have to do the original task plus the additional compensatory work. And depending on the nature of the task, avoidance may lead to a consequence of punishment or loss. That punishment/loss may be in the form of repercussions at work, a missed opportunity, or failing to meet a goal. The chores go undone, and your lawn gets so out of control that you start to find small, vicious woodland animals in it.

Other negative consequences are related to this very cycle, where your unhelpful or incorrect assumptions or beliefs remain unchallenged, you become overly effective at making excuses for yourself, and your tolerance for psychological discomfort shrinks even more. These all perpetuate the cycle even worse.

Any positive consequences are illusory. You may actually feel better because you are sticking to your unhelpful assumptions. And you will probably get some enjoyment from your procrastination activities. They may be positive in that they feel good in the moment, but they are temporary at best. It's like shutting your eyes to avoid the bright headlights of a truck barreling toward you—you are just setting yourself up for failure in the long term. It's self-sabotage.

Both sets of consequences contribute to furthering the cycle. Negative consequences make you want to continue avoiding certain tasks, while positive consequences inject just enough short-term pleasure to disguise what's really happening. And they both lead you right back to the initial problem of sitting on your butt.

You can now see how this can become a vicious cycle. The more you subscribe to one or more of the unhelpful assumptions, the greater your discomfort. With increasing discomfort, you start to make excuses to avoid. The more you avoid, the more you *want* to avoid it due to both the negative and positive consequences. And you start back in with the unhelpful assumptions—probably strengthened for the worst at this point.

So what do these phases look like in a day-to-day life situation? Let's walk through the familiar chain reaction of events that you have unwittingly followed for years. What if you've always wanted to open an ice cream shop? Your friends and family know you love ice cream, and you're always talking about this dream of yours, but you've never taken the plunge to start your own business. Maybe there's a cycle of procrastination contributing to your shop's absence.

What are the unhelpful assumptions you're telling yourself? A prime assumption would be about what might happen. If you quit your job and go full speed ahead with your ice cream business, you assume you'll be in poverty for the rest of your life. You assume being a business owner will be nonstop work. You assume you will lose a ton of money. You may even assume that you aren't smart enough to pull it off.

Thinking about these assumptions probably has you feeling pretty uncomfortable. You likely have some anxiety about such a big change. There may be some fear mixed in at the thought of quitting your job to go out on your own. You may be feeling overwhelmed by all the things that go into starting your own business.

When you're feeling this uncomfortable, it's easy to come up with excuses for not moving forward. You can't open an ice cream shop because you just don't have the know-how. Maybe your excuse is that you don't know for sure if your shop will be a success. Or perhaps you feel like you don't have time to open a business.

So as a result of these excuses, you move into avoidance activities to make yourself feel better. Instead of going to the bank to find out about business loans, you watch the football game on TV instead. You get distracted. Or you get together with friends to talk about your idea instead of taking action on steps to move toward your dream. You feel productive in some non-movement way.

As for consequences of these avoidance tactics? One negative consequence may be that you miss out on an opportunity for a perfect location for your ice cream shop because you hadn't moved forward with your plan. One positive consequence could be that you enjoy spending time with your friends and you like talking about your idea, leading you to do this more frequently instead of starting up your business. Again, negative consequences create pessimism, while positive consequences create self-sabotage.

And here we are again at the start of the cycle as a couch potato. Obviously, awareness is a sizable part of the solution. If you can honestly admit to yourself that you are engaging in this cycle, you can gain self-awareness and put a stop to it.

With regard to the five steps of the cycle, you can't necessarily control the second (increasing discomfort) and fifth (consequences). The other steps (assumptions, excuses, and actions) are where we falter, and those you *can* control.

What are your assumptions based on?

- Are they legitimate?
- Are they realistic or far-fetched?
- Are they simply your anxieties and fears taking hold?
- Are you marginalizing the positives and amplifying the downsides?

What excuses do you tend to make?

- Are they based in reality?
- Are they honest and true?
- Is their sole purpose to keep you from action?
- If your excuse was true, would it excuse you from action anyway?

What actions do you tend to engage in?

- Do you *really* want to engage in them, or are they aimed at making you feel better about yourself?
- Is there something harder you should be doing instead?
- In an ideal world, what would you be doing right now?

Unfortunately, self-awareness is not a strong point for humans. But trying to acknowledge and buttress these entry points into the cycle of procrastination can help you succeed.

The Lizard Brain

Since the time of ancient civilizations, our ancestors have struggled with the dilemma of choosing to do what needs to be done over other, usually more pleasant, activities. We may imagine that our less industrious forebearers must have had days when they relaxed, lying under a tree shade instead of picking up their spears to hunt or their baskets to forage for food. Hesiod, a Greek poet who lived around 800 B.C., cautioned not to "put your work off till tomorrow and the day after." Roman consul Cicero was also an early dissenter against procrastination, calling the act "hateful" in the conduct of affairs.

This is clearly a problem that is older than we give it credit for. Procrastination has been around since time immemorial. Has it been hardwired in our brains from the beginning?

Neurobiologists have found evidence that *yes*, the fundamental workings of our brains offer a recipe for procrastination. Procrastination is *preferred*.

Remember that procrastination is the act of delaying an intended important task despite knowing that there will be negative consequences as a result of it. We have no problem recognizing that procrastinating is likely to be bad for us. Our human logic knows procrastinating is bad, but our human impulses are often stronger and so automatic that willpower or awareness alone can't save us from indulging them.

Procrastination is a failure of self-regulation. But why do we fail to regulate ourselves? Doesn't self-regulation improve our abilities to survive and hunt and work hard for a dollar? It does, but that's a modern conception; in the past, our survival came more from a dichotomy of seeking pleasure and avoiding pain (both of which procrastination handily delivers). We are ruled by these two factors more than we like to believe.

Imagine the brain as having two major portions—an inner portion and an outer portion. The inner portion is what some scientists call our "lizard brain," responsible for our most basic survival instincts. This region is fully developed from birth and controls our most primitive drives (e.g., hunger, thirst, and sex drive), as well as our mood and emotions (e.g., fear, anger, and pleasure). It's one of the most dominant portions of our brain, as its processes tend to be automatic, not to mention life-maintaining. This portion is called the limbic system. It quite literally keeps us alive because we don't have to consciously think about breathing or becoming hungry.

This part of your brain and its associated functions evolved first in our deepest history and is many hundreds of millions of years older than our "higher brains"—the structures of which have still not evolved in countless other species. Think about this: the oldest part of your brain is the automatic unconscious part. The part that functions one hundred percent without things like willpower and intention. If we do nothing, we default to this mode. We only lift ourselves out of this mode when we actively, consciously choose to do so. In other words, we cannot simply hope to find our way to greater productivity and motivation by sheer accident or luck. We need to use the conscious part of our brains to *make* it happen.

Enter the brain's outer portion, enclosing the limbic system and situated just behind our forehead, which is called the prefrontal cortex. While the limbic system has been dubbed our "lizard brain," the prefrontal cortex has been identified by neurobiologists as the portion that separates us humans from lesser animals. The prefrontal cortex is in charge of our rational human functions, such as assimilating information, planning, making decisions, and other higher-order thinking skills.

So while the limbic system just lets us experience instincts and emotions automatically, the prefrontal cortex requires us to put in conscious and deliberate effort to be able to think, plan, decide, and ultimately complete a task. The prefrontal cortex works much, much slower, and we are generally conscious of these thoughts.

By now, you may recognize how these two major portions of the brain must be continually engaged in battle—a battle that you feel most intensely when you're faced with something you would rather not do but have to. In instances such as these, your limbic system is screaming, *"Don't do it! It doesn't feel good! WATCH TELEVISION!"* while your prefrontal cortex is trying to reason with you: *"Now, now, let's be reasonable; you have to do this."*

It's akin to what the well-known psychologist Sigmund Freud described as a constant battle between the instinctive, pleasure-driven id and the rational, reality-based ego. While the id cares only that you satisfy your impulses immediately, the ego has to consider the entire situation and the possible consequences of heeding the id's whims.

Thus, what experts are pointing to as the foundation of procrastination—the inability to manage drives and impulses—pertains to the inability of our prefrontal cortex to win over the whiny and spur-of-the-moment demands of our limbic system. The moment our prefrontal cortex lets up, we lose focus on a certain task and our limbic system is then quick to take the reins (remember, it's more automatic), moving us toward doing something more pleasurable instead.

Once we engage in that alternate activity, a chemical known as dopamine floods our brains. This is what creates the rush of pleasure we feel, and it's pretty addictive, too. We are drawn to activities that stimulate actual dopamine release, as well as to those activities we perceive will likely lead to that dopamine rush.

In other words, what leads us to procrastinate is not just the *actual* pleasure from those activities but, more importantly, the pleasure we *expect* to feel in choosing those activities over another. This is the scientific explanation behind procrastination—we anticipate we're going to feel better doing something else, so we go ahead and do it.

Our expectation of feeling good if we procrastinate is what drives us to put off our intended tasks for the moment and engage in a different activity instead. This anticipation of pleasure is the mental equivalent of drooling over a sumptuous dish; it whets our appetite for biting into the shiny yet poisoned fruit that is procrastination. Goodbye, homework; hello, old episodes of *I Love Lucy*.

If you are particularly work-shy, don't think that it's because you're a hopeless, lazy bum. Your limbic system might just be extra cunning, or your prefrontal cortex just needs a little more tweaking and practice in taking control of the situation (or both). See, your prefrontal cortex is like a muscle that can be trained and exercised to get better at beating procrastination. You can teach it to run strategies that'll boost your willpower to help you start and stay on task, jump past temptations, and hit the bullseye on your target goals.

The more primitive lizard brain is not anything to scoff at, though. It helped our ancestors evolve into the human beings we are today, and it constantly works hard in the background to keep you safe and in equilibrium. It's lightning quick and able to preserve your life at a rate hundreds of times swifter than your higher brain could ever manage. The trouble is when we allow this part of our brain to do work it wasn't designed to. The lizard brain is good for saving our lives in emergency situations and regulating our autonomous physical bodies. It's a master of impulse. It is NOT good at making long-term decisions, weighing up abstract pros and cons, and delaying gratification.

Driven by Impulse

Let's look closer at this way of acting. Impulsivity means acting immediately, whether it be a passing thought, a sudden emotion, or an instantaneous desire. Consider the common procrastination habits you may have. When you're bored with a task, it may occur to you how nice it would be to grab a bite first and relax watching an episode of your favorite sitcom, and the next second, you've abandoned your work and plopped down in front of the TV with a bag of chips.

Procrastination may have many other ways of manifesting other than that, but its many faces all have one thing in common: they arise out of an itch to do what feels good. Itches can be resisted, but not always and not forever.

If you recall, there's a constant battle between your limbic system's strong desire to seek pleasure and avoid pain and your prefrontal cortex's rational planning and decision-making controls. But while the prefrontal cortex's tasks require conscious effort to carry out, the limbic system's impulses are primitive and automatic. Unless your prefrontal cortex has been training for years and earned a black belt in limbic system control, it's likely to lose the fight against the more compelling and instinctive impulses of the limbic system.

Impulsivity is characterized by four broad characteristics, as detailed by behavioral researchers Martial Van der Linden and Mathieu d'Acremont in a 2005 study published in *The Journal of Nervous and Mental Disease*.

First, impulsivity involves **urgency**. You feel that you need to be in a rush to do something right this moment. For instance, you may feel compelled to check your social media accounts right now, and delaying it only fills you with mounting tension.

Second, there's **lack of premeditation**. You act without thinking or planning your actions, often with a relative disregard toward how such actions will affect you in the future. For example, even though you've just taken a break, you agree to a colleague's spontaneous invitation to another coffee break because you're finding your current task to be too monotonous. You fail to appreciate how unnecessarily taking yet another fifteen minutes off-task is bound to affect the progress, timeliness, and quality of your work.

Third, there's **lack of perseverance**. You easily lose motivation and are prone to giving up on tasks that require prolonged effort. For instance, instead of staying at your desk long enough to finish the inventory report you're supposed to accomplish before lunch, you lose steam halfway through and spend the rest of the morning chatting with your workmates.

And fourth, impulsivity is characterized by **sensation-seeking**. You crave that feel-good sensation that comes from engaging in activities that you find thrilling, enjoyable, or exciting. For example, you can't sit still and endure the monotony of typing out data on a computer because you're itching to go online and experience the thrill of playing *World of Warcraft* again.

Now, add those four characteristics together—urgency, lack of premeditation, lack of perseverance, and sensation-seeking—and what you get is a person who's quickly derailed from working on their intended task and instead follows their spur-of-the-moment desires. The stronger these four tendencies are in you, the more likely you'll set aside what you need to do in order to go for what feels good at the moment.

It doesn't matter that you've planned to do a task for weeks. The only thing that matters to you at that very instant is that you get to do what you feel like doing. Your new impulse feels just as urgent to you as the intended task you've known about for weeks.

Impulsivity is a key feature of a number of mental disorders, such as attention-deficit/hyperactivity disorder (ADHD), and substance abuse. People with ADHD may engage in hasty actions or decisions without first thinking of their possible consequences. For example, they may agree to do a job without knowing enough information about it, use other people's things without asking permission, or intrude into conversations by cutting others off mid-sentence. They do these things not because they want to make a fool of themselves or intend to be rude, but because they lack the ability to stop themselves from acting on their immediate impulses.

If you believe you have the tendency to be impulsive, there are certain things you can do to curb that inclination. One strategy is to use the HALT method, a popular strategy originally taught in addiction recovery programs.

Before acting or making a decision, first be conscious of any feeling of hunger, anger, loneliness, or tiredness you may have. If you're feeling any of these, you're more likely to make rash, misguided decisions and act on your impulses that may lead you right into trouble. Thus, before jumping into anything, first consider the HALT factors and address any of them that may be weakening your resolve or influencing your decision-making.

Suppose you just came out of a meeting and you're angry at one of your colleagues because he threw you under the bus for a grave error on a project you both collaborated on. You go back to your desk and try to finish another report that's due within the hour, but you feel the urge to abandon it altogether. Before you do, recognize that your impulse to procrastinate might just be triggered by your anger.

Understanding this link, you can then consider how delaying the report will only further hurt your performance standing as an employee—which, given recent events, you cannot afford to let happen. So before jumping into any rash actions, recognize that the anger pushing you to procrastinate would not be the best thing to allow at this time. You may need to calm yourself first and change your perspective of the situation in order to regain control of yourself and not give in to procrastination.

Another strategy to help you be less impulsive is to recall the benefits of delaying gratification and perform a cost-benefit analysis for waiting. Before doing this, remember that you need to clear the HALT factors first so that your ability to consider the benefits of waiting won't be compromised. No one would want to wait any longer if they were hungry, angry, lonely, or tired. Once you've established that you're free of HALT, consider how waiting at present would benefit you in the future.

For instance, imagine you're torn between completing a marketing plan summary at the office and bolting from work for three hours to catch a movie with your friends. While the prospect of relaxing in front of the big screen while sharing popcorn with your hilarious friends is definitely enticing, first recall the benefits of resisting that temptation and sticking with your task instead.

If you stay, you'll avoid getting into trouble at work, be able to cross off a major task from your to-do list, and get to fully enjoy the movie later instead of having to watch it while worried sick you might incur the wrath of your boss. Thus, delaying gratification appears to be the better option.

Nine Procrastination Scales

We've gone through how the procrastination cycle and the lizard brain affect your work ethic, and now we can talk about some specific traits that need to be addressed and shored up.

Noting the connection between procrastination and the prefrontal cortex, researcher Laura Rabin of Brooklyn College delved into a closer examination of the relationship between procrastination and major processes in the prefrontal cortex.

Rabin's study assessed a sample of 212 students for procrastination, as well as the nine clinical subscales of prefrontal cortex executive functioning: (1) inhibition, (2) self-monitoring, (3) planning and organization, (4) activity shifting, (5) task initiation, (6) task monitoring, (7) emotional control, (8) working memory, and (9) general orderliness.

The researchers expected the first four of these subscales to be linked to procrastination. As it turned out, the results exceeded their expectations—all nine subscales were found to have significant associations with procrastination, as reported by Rabin and her colleagues in a 2011 issue of the *Journal of Clinical and Experimental Neuropsychology*.

Let's consider how each of these nine executive functions relates to procrastination. Perhaps you'll be able to identify yourself in some of them.

Inhibition. This pertains to your ability to be "in control" of yourself, to resist impulses, and to stop your own behavior when it's appropriate to do so. Inability to perform this function well leads to impulsivity, which typically manifests as acting without thinking. If you're prone to acting without first considering the consequences of your actions, then you might have problems with inhibition.

Lack of inhibition is a key factor in procrastination. If you can't control yourself enough to resist the impulse of going for an easier, more pleasurable activity, then you'll always just be choosing to do virtually anything else other than what you're supposed to be doing. You'll always be giving in to the temptation to engage in a more enjoyable activity rather than taking the pains of sticking to your to-do list.

Say you've intended to spend your first hour at the office researching ideas for your marketing proposal. However, as you sit down to work on it, your phone keeps beeping with notifications from the lively social media scene. Lacking inhibitory control, you fail to resist checking your phone and engaging with your friends on social media, and thus you end up procrastinating on your intended research task.

Self-monitoring. This refers to your ability to monitor your own behavior and its effect on you. Taken to the extreme, it's like being able to watch yourself from a bird's-eye view and understand why you are acting in certain ways.

Impaired self-monitoring thus inevitably results in a severe lack of self-awareness. It means you can't think about your own thinking, and thus you can be ruled by your lizard brain without even being aware of it. When lacking such self-awareness and the ability to think about your thinking, you'll be more likely to fall prey to destructive patterns of thought and bad habits, including procrastination.

When you're unaware of how you behave, you'll be less likely to even realize you're procrastinating. This is what happens when we pick up our phone to check an email and suddenly an hour of scrolling on social media passes.

Planning and organization. This comprises your ability to manage present and future task demands. The planning component of this function is about your ability to set goals and map out the right order of steps to get the job done. The organization component pertains to your ability to pick up on the main ideas of a given information load and to bring order to information. Together, planning and organization involve your ability to anticipate future situations and demands accurately and to take those into account as you lay out the steps necessary to achieve your goals.

If you lack the ability to set realistic goals and establish plans to meet those goals, you'll fail to understand the work and time needed.

As an example, imagine you need to work on completing a financial report due two weeks from now. Lacking effective planning skills, you don't break down the task into smaller portions and don't set specific hours you're going to work on it. You simply go through the days doing whatever's pushed under your nose (fonts, formatting, and type of paper to print on) and relaxing when nothing's due on that day. You put off doing the report until you realize, much to your panic, that it's due in two hours' time.

Activity shifting. This reflects your ability to easily move from one activity to another. If you're adept at activity shifting, you can make transitions effortlessly and tolerate change without getting distracted and off-track. This function also involves your ability to switch or alternate your attention as needed and to shift your focus from one aspect of a problem to another. Consider this your ability to be flexible in terms of both behavior and thinking.

A deficit in activity-shifting ability is linked with procrastination. After all, getting down to work basically constitutes a shift from non-working to working mode. If you're unable to switch from rest mode or from one productive mode to another, then you'll end up procrastinating because you just can't get yourself to switch to the other side. You'll stagnate at your original state, either doing nothing or continuing an activity you're not supposed to be doing at the time.

Say you've been diligent enough to draw up a schedule for the day. You've written that you're going to do some gardening from 8:00 a.m. to 9:00 a.m., then move inside the house and work on a manuscript from 9:00 a.m. to 11:00 a.m. However, you're fully enjoying and so engrossed in your gardening that you continue with it well past the time you've set for it to stop.

You end up spending your entire morning just gardening because you lacked the ability to shift your focus and energy onto the next task as scheduled. This form of procrastination can be tricky to spot and address, as it can look like you're making good use of your time when in fact you're not.

Task initiation. This pertains to your ability to simply start and get going on tasks or activities. It is what enables you to break the inertia of inactivity and take the first step on the task at hand—or on any task, for that matter. The first step is always the toughest to take. Task initiation also includes your capacity to generate ideas and problem-solving strategies by yourself. If this function is weak, you'll find it very difficult to begin anything. It will feel like you can see a long, winding road stretching out before you, but you just can't lift your foot to take the first step and walk along it.

You set a "start time" for each of your intended tasks, but once that moment arrives, you always find a reason to reschedule the start to another time. Or you just continue engaging in other activities you find more enjoyable.

It's 8:30 a.m. You say, *"I'll start at 9:00 a.m."* When you look back at the clock, you see it's

9:15 a.m. So you figure, *"Nah, I'll start at 10:00 a.m."* This carries on until oblivion.

Task monitoring. This refers to your ability to evaluate and keep track of your projects, as well as to identify and correct mistakes in your work. This also includes your ability to judge how easy or difficult a task will be for you and whether your problem-solving approaches are working or not. If your task monitoring function is impaired, you'll likely find it difficult to weed out which tasks need to be done first, or you may forget what you need to do altogether.

Deficient task monitoring is associated with procrastination. If you lack the ability to track your tasks, you'll fail to prioritize your activities properly, leading you to focus on the less important stuff. What's more, if you misjudge the difficulty of a certain task, you're more likely to put it off until later because you expect it to be easier than it actually is. A more realistic evaluation of the time and effort a task requires is essential to avoiding procrastination.

For instance, say you have a bunch of supply requests to review and approve. You estimate that it will take about an hour to finish all of them, and you've scheduled yourself to do the task during your last hour in the office.

However, when that hour arrives, you don't feel motivated to proceed, so you put it off until tomorrow. After all, it will just take an hour.

Eventually, your attention is called as you've delayed the task for several days already and more work is piling up. When you finally sit down to work, you realize you've underestimated the time it takes to complete the task and regret all the time you wasted procrastinating.

Emotional control. This encompasses your ability to modulate or regulate your emotional responses. When your emotional control function is on point, you're able to react to events and situations appropriately. On the other hand, when your emotional control is problematic, you're likely to overreact to small problems, have sudden or frequent mood changes, get emotional easily, or have inappropriate outbursts.

Such inability to control your emotions is also likely to negatively impact your ability to control your thoughts. Emotions that run wild can derail the train of thought of even the most rational and intelligent people. So if you can't keep a lid on your emotions, you can't expect to be in full control of your thoughts—and your resulting actions—as well.

Remember the limbic system, that part of your brain that plays a significant role in your emotions, drives, and instincts? You're practically handing it the reins to direct your behavior if you lack the ability to control your emotional responses.

Imagine how a baby behaves. Because it's not yet adept at emotional control, it mostly just responds to the whims of the limbic system (e.g., when it's hungry, it cries without regard for appropriateness of time and place).

Let's say you're trying to work out solutions for a financial problem at the company. This undertaking is important but is causing you so much mental fatigue and distress that you decide to set it aside and pick up that entertaining phone of yours instead. The result? Procrastination.

Working memory. This comprises your capacity to hold information in your mind long enough to be able to complete a task. Your working memory is what enables you to follow complex instructions, manipulate information in your mind (e.g., do mental calculations), and carry out activities that have multiple steps. If you've ever walked into a room and forgotten what you went there for, you've experienced a lapse in your working memory. Scientists routinely estimate average working memory at having a capacity of *seven plus or minus two items.*

Poor working memory equals procrastination because you will literally forget what you are working on and why. It also lets you be more affected by temptations and distractions in your environment. You may have difficulty maintaining your attention on tasks that have multiple steps, leading you to stop halfway through and procrastinate instead.

Say you're tasked to review records of your project expenditures and prepare a progress report to inform upper management of your current project status. You had no problem getting yourself started on the task, but after looking over a couple of financial reports, you're finding it hard to keep track of the connections between all the papers you've been reading. Unable to remain focused, you shift your attention to the office chatter happening at the next cubicle. The next thing you know, you've joined your coworkers' conversation and have successfully abandoned your task for the day.

General orderliness. This refers to your ability to keep the things you need for projects well-organized and readily available, as well as to keep your workspaces orderly so that you're able to find whatever you need when you need it. General orderliness brings about efficiency in the way you work, as it allows you to spend less time looking for things and more time actually working on the task.

If your work area or living space is not well-organized, you'll be more likely to find yourself in situations when you need to get up from working and look for things or even go out and buy materials you forgot you needed. You'll have veritable invitations for procrastination staring you in the face every moment of the day.

Distracted by these additional activities, you'll be more tempted to delay what you should be doing and instead engage in trivial activities. This applies even to the organization of files in your computer. If in your attempt to find one document, you need to sift through piles of folders with no discernable organizational scheme to them whatsoever, you're likely to come across other stuff that will distract you and lead you to procrastinate.

As a brief review, procrastination may arise from problems in each of the nine executive functions: (1) inhibition, (2) self-monitoring, (3) planning and organization, (4) activity shifting, (5) task initiation, (6) task monitoring, (7) emotional control, (8) working memory, and (9) general orderliness.

Some people may have a habit of procrastinating because they have trouble stopping themselves from engaging in certain activities (inhibition), others may procrastinate because they find it challenging to start (task initiation), and so on. Whatever the case, as with the previous section on the cycle of procrastination, it is imperative to understand what leads you to that point. Only then do solutions have a chance of being successful.

More often than not, procrastination can easily get out of hand and slowly eat away at your chances of achieving professional success and personal satisfaction. So how do you prevent procrastination from wreaking havoc in your life? Well, first things first: you've got to recognize the warning signs.

Takeaways:

- Procrastination has been around far longer than you or me. The term "procrastination" was derived from the Latin *pro*, meaning "forward, forth, or in favor of" and *crastinus*, meaning "of tomorrow." In everyday terms, it's when you put off something unpleasant, usually in pursuit of something more pleasurable or enjoyable. In this first chapter, we discuss the typical causes of procrastination.

- This begins with the cycle of procrastination, which has five stages: unhelpful/false assumptions, increasing discomfort, excuse-making, avoidance activities, and consequences. Focus on dispelling your false assumptions, dissecting your excuses, and understanding your avoidance activities.

- The pleasure principle is important to understand in the context of procrastination. Our brains have a constant civil war brewing inside; the impulsive and largely subconscious lizard brain wants immediate pleasure at the expense of the slower prefrontal cortex, which makes rational decisions. The prefrontal cortex makes the unpopular decisions that procrastination is not a fan of, while the lizard brain makes decisions that lead to dopamine and adrenaline being produced. It may seem like a losing battle, but the key to battling procrastination is being able to regulate our impulses and drives—though not suppress them.

- You might simply be an impulsive person. Four traits make up impulsivity: urgency (I must do this right now), lack of premeditation (I don't know how this will affect me later), lack of perseverance (I'm tired of this; what else is there to do?), and sensation-seeking (oh, that feels better than what I am currently doing). The more elevated your levels, the more impulsive and procrastinating you will be.

- A helpful method for defeating procrastination is called HALT, and it stands for hunger, anger, loneliness, or tiredness. When you are facing a fork in the road in regards to persevering or procrastinating, ask yourself if any of the HALT factors are present. If any are, understand that you are already predisposed to making a poor decision and try to regulate your thoughts.
- It's been found that there are nine specific traits associated with procrastination: (1) inhibition, (2) self-monitoring, (3) planning and organization, (4) activity shifting, (5) task initiation, (6) task monitoring, (7) emotional control, (8) working memory, and (9) general orderliness. Generally, deficiencies in any of these nine traits will make an individual more susceptible to procrastination. To beat procrastination, we must perform one of the hardest tasks of all: thinking about one's own thinking.

Chapter 2: Action Mindsets

"If and When were planted, and Nothing grew."
—Proverb

At this point, you've learned why you are engaging in procrastination. You should be able to generally identify a few reasons that you are a couch potato, aka someone who lacks focus and productivity. It might be due to your prefrontal cortex being hijacked by your lizard brain, or it might be due to being unknowingly immersed in the procrastination cycle. You may have even identified one or two typologies in yourself. But whatever the case, the time begins for real solutions.

This chapter entails building anti-procrastination mindsets—outlooks and approaches that get you off your butt to deal with the options you come across in more productive ways. As we've seen, conscious intention and awareness is the first step. Once you know *why* and *how* your productivity is lacking, you can start making intelligent and informed decisions toward fulfilling your real potential. Then, it becomes a question of adapting the right mindset and using the right tools.

There are at least three ways you can build a mindset that's iron-clad against the ever-constant lure of procrastination: (1) mastering the physics of productivity, (2) eliminating the paradox of choice, and (3) finding the right motivation to kickstart action.

The Physics of Productivity

Who would have thought that productivity and procrastination could be viewed through the lens of physics, math, and equations? Bestselling author Stephen Guise found a way to do so using Newton's three laws of motion as an analogy to formulate the Three Laws of Productivity.

By dissecting procrastination as physics concepts and equations with identifiable elements and interactions, you'll get to identify the specific things you need to do or to avoid in order to add to your productivity and subtract from your procrastination. If you know the variables at work when you procrastinate, then you'll literally be able to single out a particular variable and manipulate it as you're able to do in a mathematical equation.

The three laws of motion were formulated by physicist Sir Isaac Newton in 1687 to explain how physical objects and systems move and are affected by the forces around them. He's the guy who claims to have conceived of gravity after getting hit by a falling apple. These laws lay the foundation for understanding how things from the smallest machine parts to the largest spacecraft and planets move. And now applied to the science of human cognition and behavior, these laws can also illuminate the mechanisms behind procrastination—and how to manipulate those mechanisms to drive productivity instead.

First law of motion. According to Newton's first law of motion, an object at rest tends to remain at rest and an object in motion continues to be in motion unless an outside force acts upon it.

How this law applies to procrastination is glaringly evident: an object at rest tends to remain at rest, which means a person in a state of rest tends to remain at rest—unless some sort of force moves him or her into action. So if you're currently in a state of inaction with regard to your intended task, you'll tend to remain inactive unless you're stimulated into motion. Your tendency to leave that task untouched is thus a fundamental law of the universe.

But before you start to think being a perpetual procrastinator is a hopeless case, remember that Newton's first law of motion works the other way, too: an object in motion continues to be in motion, which means a person in a state of action tends to continue moving as well. So if you're currently working on a task, this law of motion states that you'll tend to keep working on that task.

So what does this mean in the context of productivity and procrastination? The most critical element of beating procrastination is to find a way to start. Find a way to get moving. Once you get the ball rolling, it gets infinitely easier to keep going until the task is done.

Now, the next question becomes, how do you get started on a task? Writer James Clear suggests following what's known as the two-minute rule as applied to productivity. The rule states that you need to start your task in less than two minutes from the time you start thinking about it. Think of it as a personal contract you strike with yourself. No matter what, you need to start within the next two minutes.

For example, suppose you're tasked to write a report detailing your department's project updates. To beat the inertia of lazing around the entire morning, commit to just jotting down the project title and objectives or expected output within the next two minutes. You don't need to think about doing the rest of it just yet. You only need to start within the next two minutes. This action will help break the inactivity that's been strapping you down, and once you've started writing things down about your project, you'll find it easier to keep going.

Another benefit of abiding by this rule is that you'll also be forced to break the task down into smaller and smaller steps, as giving yourself a two-minute limit for starting requires you to think in terms of more manageable chunks of work you can start quick and easy.

Note that the two-minute rule doesn't require you to pledge that you finish your task or even proceed with your task in an orderly manner. It doesn't need you to mind the quality of your output just yet; you can reserve the critiquing and refining of it for later. It just needs you to start, to get into motion.

This relieves a lot of the pressure that typically paralyzes you from touching a task and thus leads you down a path of procrastination. With Newton's first law of motion, you'll find that once you start, you will tend to keep going on your task. So rather than wait for an enormous amount of motivation before starting, just go ahead and start small. You'll find that your motivation will snowball into ever-larger amounts after you've started.

Second law of motion. Newton's second law of motion explains how a particular force affects the rate at which an object is moving. It is represented by the equation $F=ma$, which states that the sum of forces (F) acting on an object is the product of that object's mass (m, which refers to how much matter there is in an object) and its acceleration (a, which is the rate of change in how fast an object is going).

In other words, the second law of motion dictates how much force is needed in order to accelerate an object of a particular mass in a certain direction. And as illustrated by the equation, the relationship between these three variables—force, mass, and acceleration—is proportional. The greater the mass of an object, the greater the force required to accelerate it. Likewise, the faster you need an object to move over time (i.e., accelerate), the greater the force you'll need to apply.

So if you want to accelerate an object—say, a ball—then the amount of force you exert on that ball, as well as the direction of that force you apply on the ball, will both make a difference. If more force is applied for the ball to go left than for it to go right, then you can bet that ball will go left.

Still with me?

Applied to productivity, this means that you'll need to pay attention not only to the amount of work you're doing (magnitude), but also to where you're applying that work (direction). If you work a lot but don't focus all that work in a single direction, then you'll tend to accomplish less than when you direct the same amount of work to only one direction.

The amount of work you're able to do as a person has its limits, so if you want to get the most out of your effort, you need to start being conscious of where that work goes. As Newton's $F=ma$ equation teaches, where you direct your effort is just as important as how much effort you exert. Temptations, distractions, and lack of task prioritization all serve to scatter your energy and effort in different directions, so avoiding them is key to optimizing your productivity. Keep your energy focused.

Say you have a myriad of things to accomplish before the day is up—reply to five client emails, read and critique a lengthy research plan, and write a recommendation letter for a former employee.

Applying Newton's second law, you need to recognize that how fast you'll be able to accomplish a particular task depends largely on your ability to focus the effort you exert on that task and that task only. If you insist on scattering the "force" you exert by frequently switching tabs from email to research to letter-writing all throughout the morning, you'll be less likely to accomplish any one of them before the lunch hour. You may even just be switching back and forth on those tasks as a way to procrastinate on all of them.

To remedy this, apply the principle of Newton's second law: exert your force in a single direction for its maximum acceleration.

Third law of motion. This law of motion states that "for every action, there is an equal and opposite reaction." This means that when Object A applies a force on Object B, Object B simultaneously applies a force of the same amount, but of opposite direction, on Object A. For example, when you swim, you apply force on the water as you push it backward.

Simultaneously, the water applies a force on you that's equal in magnitude yet opposite in direction, thus pushing you forward.

Applied to the science of productivity and procrastination, this law reflects how in your own life there are often productive and unproductive forces at work as well. There is a constant battle, and everyone's level of balance is different. For those who are unproductive, their unproductive forces tend to win more often than not.

Productive forces include positivity, atmosphere, environment, social network, focus, and motivation, while unproductive forces include stress, temptation and distraction, unrealistic work goals, and unhealthy lifestyles (e.g., poor diet or lack of sleep). The interaction and balance between these opposite forces is what creates your typical levels of productivity, as well as your usual patterns of procrastination.

This balance could shift either way—it could lead you to be massively productive or to severely procrastinate. For example, it may take you just an hour to finish writing a report when you're feeling well-rested and confident in your abilities, but you may need a week to complete the same task when you're feeling stressed out and insecure.

Basing on the applications of Newton's third law of motion, there are two ways you can go about upping your productivity level and avoid procrastination. The first is to add more productive forces. This is what James Clear refers to as the "power through it" option, in which you simply find a way to pump yourself up with more energy in an attempt to overpower the unproductive forces inhibiting you from working. This strategy may involve such actions as chugging cup after cup of coffee and digesting motivational words through books or inspirational videos.

The "power through it" option could work well, but only for a brief time. The problem with this strategy is that you're only trying to cover up the unproductive forces that are still working to undermine your productivity, and this tiring task could easily lead to burnout.

As an alternative, Clear suggests dealing with unproductive forces directly through the second option, which is to subtract, if not totally eliminate, unproductive forces. This strategy involves such actions as reducing the number of tasks you commit to, learning how to say no, and changing your environment in order to simplify your life.

Compared to the first option, which requires you to add more productive forces, this second option simply needs you to release the reservoir of energy and productivity already within you by removing the barriers that obstruct it. As you can imagine, this second option is an easier way to defeat procrastination than having to produce productivity by attempting to add more productive forces.

For example, say you need to accomplish a year-end evaluation report for your organization's project sponsor. You're aware that you're the type of worker who needs quiet in order to think and work effectively, but your office cubicle is between two chatty colleagues. Instead of simply opting to "power through" the task despite the noisy and distracting environment you're in (i.e., attempting to increase your productive forces), consider relocating to a quieter area or politely asking your colleagues to refrain from disturbing you for the next hour or two (i.e., eliminating unproductive forces). That way, you'll be more motivated to start and keep working on a task, not necessarily because you've upped your willpower, but because you've simply let the natural energy already within you flow unhindered.

Granted, this way of looking at things might not seem entirely a good fit for you, and that's okay. As we saw in the several stages of the procrastination cycle, not everyone's issues with focus and productivity stem from the same cause. For some people, the issue is hiding in plain sight and doesn't at first look like an issue at all: having plenty of attractive options in front of you.

Eliminate the Paradox of Choice

While most people tend to think that having choices is good—and the more choices there are, the better—current research on human behavior actually suggests otherwise. In a phenomenon that psychologist Barry Schwartz calls the paradox of choice, people tend to be worse off when they have more options to choose from as opposed to when they have a single course of action available to them. In fact, the phenomenon known as "decision fatigue" is a way to describe the paralysis and sense of uncomfortable indecision that comes from having to process too many possible options. We'll be looking at practical ways to reduce this cognitive tension in a later chapter.

To give an example of the behavior paradox and how it can cause havoc, suppose your company offers multiple types of research grants you can apply for. Pressured to make the "best" choice among all your options and overwhelmed by the details and comparisons you need to sift through to be able to do so, you put the whole research thing on the back burner and leave it untouched for years. With zero additional research studies under your belt, you suffer career stagnation simply because in the face of multiple options, you've been too paralyzed to do anything.

Learning to deal with the paradox of choice is thus a necessary technique to beat procrastination. If you've established a mindset that's able to promptly make sound decisions in the face of multiple options, then you'll less likely fall into the paralysis or stress that causes most people to procrastinate.

The paradox of choice tends to impact things negatively because once people become overwhelmed with too many options, one of two things tends to happen.

One, after making a choice, you may still constantly think about the other options that you didn't choose. For instance, after buying a painting, you may still fixate on imagining how great the other paintings you didn't buy would look in place of the one you bought. So you're never really satisfied with the choices you make because a part of you remains preoccupied with thoughts of all the other options you missed out on by making a choice. It is the ultimate case of buyer's remorse.

Two, having too many options can subject you to a very difficult time deciding, such that you become paralyzed from making a decision and from doing anything at all. In philosophy, this is illustrated by the paradox of Buridan's ass (quite literally, donkey). Popularized by philosopher Jean Buridan, this paradox tells of a hungry donkey standing between two identical piles of hay. The donkey always chooses the hay closer to him, but this time both piles are of equal distance away. Unable to choose between the two piles, the donkey starves to death.

Applied to the mechanisms of work and productivity, the paradox of choice thus ultimately leads you to procrastinate, as you delay making a decision or starting on a task in an attempt to avoid the overwhelming pressure you feel from having so many options. The availability of options creates the illusion of greater personal responsibility to make not only the right choice, but the best one.

To beat the paradox of choice, the key is to set rules and restraints upon yourself. You'll need to find a way to see things in black and white, because gray areas are fertile grounds that breed overthinking and procrastination. That spectrum of gray is likely to see you get stuck and agonize over which shade of gray is the best choice until you get tired of the uncertainty, lose motivation, and end up being paralyzed from making any choice and acting at all. When Buridan's donkey saw shades of gray instead of one defined path to one defined dish of food, he faltered and ultimately starved to death.

To avoid falling into that trap, use the following strategies.

Focus on one factor and willfully ignore everything else. Every option is sure to offer its own pros and cons, and deciding among numerous options is not merely a matter of tabulating which has the most pros and the least cons. Rather, making a choice depends heavily on what you really care about, which often boils down to only one or two critical factors. So instead of having to deal with countless criteria that can overwhelm you from making a choice, focus only on one or two vital factors and ignore the rest. That way, you have a clearer idea about which option is best for you, and you can select it faster, too.

Suppose you need to buy a new microwave and have multiple models lined up in front of you, each with its own set of features and unique innovations. If you don't know which factors you want to focus on, it's easy to get confused by all the bells and whistles that such a large selection offers.

So to make it easier for you to make a choice that's really suited to your needs, decide beforehand on one or two specific features you want to mainly base your choice on—say, size (i.e., must fit your kitchen space) and sensor cooking. With just these two features in mind, you get to eliminate a lot of other models that don't fit the bill, thus effectively narrowing down your choices to make it easier for you to select the right one.

Set a time limit on making a decision. Commit to making a decision within, say, two minutes tops. Whatever decision you arrive at by the end of two minutes, stick with it no matter what. This defeats the paradox of choice by putting a cap on the amount of time you spend agonizing over which decision to make. It saves you from suffering the negative consequences of letting things pass you by and spurs you into the action necessary to realize your goals.

For example, imagine you're in charge of choosing and facilitating the venue for your upcoming gala but you're torn between Venue A and Venue B. You've put off making reservations for weeks now simply because you can't decide which venue would be the better choice. To save yourself from wasting any more time procrastinating, set two minutes for you to come up with a decision and pledge to stick with it.

You may go back and forth between the two venues within those two minutes, but once the time is up, whatever venue you settle on should be the one you go for—say, Venue A. To strengthen this strategy (no backsies!), make sure to call and make reservations for Venue A by the end of the two minutes.

Immediately choose a default option and stick with it if no better alternative comes up. Once you've selected one option as the default, you can set a short amount of time to try to find alternatives and weigh them against your default choice. If none of the alternatives measure up to your default, then you just revert to that default choice. That way, you're ensured of having already made a decision beforehand, which you can simply follow through with once it's time to act.

The fact that you've chosen a default already constitutes a choice in itself, one that you'll most likely be inclined to stick with and follow through on.

For example, again imagine you're in charge of choosing the venue for your upcoming gala, but you're so torn between Venue A and Venue B that you've put off facilitating the task altogether.

To save yourself from further procrastinating, you may set Venue A as your default choice, then allow three days for you to continue searching for other alternatives or to continue comparing the pros and cons between Venue A and Venue B. If by the end of the third day you find yourself either unconvinced by the other options or so convinced by all of them you're now confused, then just revert to your default choice of Venue A. That way, you can start moving on with the rest of your event planning instead of getting stuck and procrastinating because you can't make a choice. Training your mind to select a default option preps it to be more inclined toward active decision-making rather than toward the passivity and paralysis that breeds procrastination habits.

Finally, strive to satisfice your desires more often than not. The word *satisfice* is a combination of the words *satisfy* and *suffice*. It's a term that Herbert Simon coined in the 1950s, and it represents what we should shoot for rather than something that is guaranteed to optimize and maximize our happiness.

Generally, people can be split into those two categories: those who seek to satisfice a decision and those who seek to maximize a decision.

Let's suppose that you are shopping for a new bike. The maximizer would devote hours to researching their decision and evaluating as many options as possible. They would want to get the best one possible for their purposes and want to leave no stone unturned. They want one hundred percent satisfaction despite the law of diminishing returns and the Pareto principle, which would warn against such measures.

By contrast, the satisficer is just shooting to be satisfied and is looking for an option that suffices for their purposes. They want something that works well enough to make them satisfied and pleased but not overjoyed or ecstatic. They aim for *good enough* and stop once they find that.

These are very different scales, and for this reason, studies have shown that satisficers tend to be happier with their decisions while maximizers tend to keep agonizing and thinking about greener pastures after their decisions.

Maximization represents a conundrum in our modern age because while it is more possible now than at any other point in human history to get exactly what you want, there is also the paradox of choice, which makes it impossible to be satisfied. On a practical matter, there are few decisions where we should strive to maximize our value. Therefore, put forth proportional effort and just make a choice already.

Most of the time, you simply want something that is reliable and works. Suppose you are in a grocery store and you are trying to pick out the type of peanut butter you want. What should you shoot for here? Satisficing or maximizing? The same type of thinking should apply to ninety-nine percent of our daily decisions. Otherwise, we are constantly overwhelmed and waste our mental bandwidth where there are diminishing returns. Whatever net benefit the most optimal type of peanut butter brings to your life is likely not worth the extra effort it took to find it.

Motivation Follows Action

One final mindset to embrace in the battle against procrastination is to consider the way in which true motivation and the appetite for productivity appears naturally . . . and when it doesn't. Most of the time, whatever the real reason is, we end up telling ourselves that if we aren't in the mood (I don't *feel* like it), then it's not getting done.

Look, it would be five-million times easier to achieve our goals if we all knew how to motivate ourselves one hundred percent of the time. It would be like pressing a magical button that jolts us out of bed and into work. Whenever our energy is faltering, we could just press the button again, and we'd be injected with another dose of that good stuff and be correspondingly productive. The closest legal thing we have to this is coffee, but even that has waning effects.

It's easier to feel motivated when you like a project or when you're doing something you are genuinely passionate about. But let's be realistic—there are days when just the mere act of leaving your bed is a challenge and a huge accomplishment. For most of us, we don't enjoy what we do enough to feel motivated by it. An artist may be inspired and motivated to bring her visions into reality, but for the rest of us? We're really just trying to scrape together enough willpower to get us through our days. This is all to clarify motivation's role in taking action and getting started.

Whatever your goals, motivation plays an important role and can spell the difference between success and failure. It's one of the most important ingredients to influence your drive and ambition, but we're thinking about it *all wrong*.

When we think about motivation, we want something that will light a spark in us and make us jump up from the couch and deeply into our tasks. We want *motivation that causes action*. There are a few problems with this, namely the fact that you're probably looking for something that doesn't exist, and that's going to keep you waiting on the sidelines, out of action and out of the race. This type of motivation, if you ever find it, is highly unreliable. If you feel that you need motivation that causes action, you are doing it wrong.

For instance, a writer who feels they are unable to write without some form of motivation or inspiration is going to stare at a blank page for hours. End of story.

The truth is, you should plan for life *without* a motivating kickstart. Seeking that motivation creates a prerequisite and additional barrier to action. Get into the habit of proceeding without it. And surprisingly, this is where you'll find what you were seeking. *Action leads to motivation*, more motivation, and eventually momentum.

The more you work for something, the more meaningful it becomes to you. Your own actions will be your fuel to move forward. After you've taken your first step and have seen progress from your efforts, motivation will come easier and more naturally, as will inspiration and discipline. You'll fall into a groove, and suddenly, you'll be in your work mood/mode. The first step will always be the hardest step, but the second step won't be.

For repetition's sake, forget motivation; get started and you'll *become* motivated. Taking the first step is tough, but consider that aside from motivation, just getting started gives you many other things.

For instance, confidence also follows action. After all, how do you expect to be confident about something when you haven't even tried? A taste of action tells you that everything will be okay and you have nothing to fear. This is confidence rooted in firsthand experience, which is easier to find as opposed to false confidence that you get from trying to convince yourself before the fact that you can do it.

Public speaking is almost always a scary proposition. Consider how you might try to find confidence that causes action: you would tell yourself it will all be fine, imagine the audience in their underwear, and remind yourself of your hours of rehearsal. Now consider how you might find confidence after getting started— how action can cause confidence. "I did it and it was fine" is an easier argument to make versus "I haven't done it yet, but I think it will be fine."

The most important takeaway here is to not wait until you are one hundred percent ready before you take the first step or that motivation is a necessary part of your process. It will probably never feel like you're completely ready. But starting down the road will motivate you more than anything else will before the fact, so allow your actions to motivate you and build confidence. Change your expectations regarding motivation and remove the self-imposed requirements you have for yourself.

As a member of the human race, the tendency for procrastination may be hardwired into your limbic system (and for good reason!) but that doesn't mean you should forever be a slave to your own primitive drives and impulses. You are also blessed with a higher mind that can take considered, conscious action for your own benefit. In other words, you can *choose*.

Waning productivity, a lack of focus or motivation, and a bad procrastination problem are signs of a complex, all-too-human condition. We've looked at three helpful alternative mindsets that you consciously choose: the scientific analog that looks at energy, one that takes into account the mental load that comes with decision-making behavior, and finally a more psychological model that focuses on our attitudes and beliefs about what "motivation" is and what that means for our choices and action.

Cultivating one or more of these mindsets in yourself will grant you better control of your unconscious limbic drives and impulses, and help you access that state of focused and fulfilled productive living.

Takeaways:

- Procrastination may be a reflection of battling biological forces, and we can swing the battle in our favor if we use some of the mindset tactics in this chapter. Fear is an understated underlying cause of procrastination.
- The first such tactic is to understand how Newton's three laws of motion can apply to procrastination. Viewing your productivity (or lack thereof) as an equation is helpful because it allows you to think through the variables present in your life and learn how to manipulate them. First, an object at rest tends to stay at rest, while an object in motion tends to stay in motion (the first step is the hardest step). Next, the amount of work produced is a product of the focus

and the force that is applied toward it (focus your efforts intentionally). Finally, for every action, there is an equal and opposite reaction (take inventory of the productive and unproductive forces present in your life).

- Another factor in procrastination is the paradox of choice, wherein choices and options are actually detrimental because they cause indecision and plague us with doubt. They might even cause us to act like Buridan's donkey and proverbially starve to death between two dishes of food. To combat this, get into the habit of setting a time limit on your decisions, making matters black and white, aiming to become satisficed, and immediately picking a default option.

- Finally, understand that motivation and the mood to stop procrastinating is not something that appears spontaneously. It may never appear . . . *before* the fact. But after you get started, it will almost always appear. Motivation *follows* action, yet most of us are seeking motivation that *creates* action. We are doing it backward and just need to get started to feel better, more often than not.

Chapter 3: Psychological Tactics

"Procrastination is the grave in which opportunity is buried."

—Anonymous

How do you get a machine to work?

You need to plug it into an energy source and push the right buttons. Now, getting yourself to work wouldn't be quite as simple as that, and you are certainly more complicated than any mere machine. But to use a less-than-perfect metaphor, you do possess certain "energy sources" you can plug into and psychological "buttons" you can push to get yourself to be more productive and avoid procrastinating.

If you know where to tap the energy to power yourself through tasks and which buttons to push—or avoid pushing—to get yourself to work, then you'll be able to beat procrastination and be well on your way to achieving your goals. Think of it this way: the couch potato is not lacking knowledge or ability for the task they're avoiding. If they were, then the simple cure for procrastination would simply be education. No, something else is missing.

Try to think of the last time that you were really fired up to do something, and procrastinating on that task was the last thing on your mind. *Why* did you find it so easy to hunker down and give it your all? What exactly allowed you to pour all your energy and attention into the task at hand and give your very best? If we can identify this X factor, we are getting closer to finding out what is missing in the couch potato's world.

This chapter will introduce you to three *psychological* tactics that'll have you push just the right buttons in your own psyche so you can get yourself up and running as you set about accomplishing your tasks, just like you have done naturally in the past. If you are having trouble with productivity and lack focus and motivation, then it's inevitable that you'll need to consider how your own psychology is hindering you. Here are four proven tactics that'll help you push all the right buttons, so to speak: (1) don't rely on your mood, (2) deal with omission bias, (3) visualize your future self, and (4) use the if-then technique.

No One Simply "Feels Like it"

How many times have you put off a task just because you're "not yet in the mood" to work on it or because you "don't feel like working"? What's your record for the length of time you've waited to "feel the right moment to start" before you actually set about on a task?

You might remember this excuse from the very first chapter, where some of us labor under the unconscious core belief that we are only required to act when we feel spontaneously and effortlessly inspired to do so, and if not, then we are off the hook and can't possibly take action. Many people may even believe that to be more productive or kill procrastination, they will need to somehow find more passion and love for their work, or listen to "motivational speakers" who will rile up the needed enthusiasm. But the truth is, *no enthusiasm is needed*. This is all just an elaborate excuse and delay tactic. Passion is nice but not necessary.

Instead of waiting for your mood to spark you into action, though, you could act first in order to spark your mood into a motivated, all-systems-go mode. In other words, we need to challenge this assumption that action requires inspiration, and instead get into the habit of taking action regardless.

Start operating under the notion that the right action inspires the right mood, instead of the other way around. For example, whether or not you feel in the mood to research that project you're supposed to do, sit yourself down and start browsing a page on the subject. Soon enough, you'll find yourself gaining more and more momentum, and you'll feel more and more motivated to keep with the task.

No matter what mood you're in—happy or cranky, excited or bored, calm or edgy—just start. You know all this, and now we go beyond the simple assertion that action is what matters. The question still remains: how do we get to that point? We can logically know that we are acting against our own interests but still remain stuck to the couch.

Researchers have designed a playbook of strategies to help you get there. The added benefit to mastering this playbook is that it will not only help you take action no matter what mood you're in, but also equip you with strategies to repair your mood in general. So whether it's your intention to kick the procrastination bug out of your system or to simply convert negative feelings into positive ones, practice the two psychological tricks described below to experience a mood boost whenever you need one.

First, set a low threshold for getting started. As advised by Dr. Timothy Pychyl, a leading researcher in the field of procrastination, making the threshold for getting started relatively low can trick your mind into getting motivated for a task. The low threshold suggests to you that the task is completely manageable, and anticipating that you'll easily get past the first hurdle of the task will help you boost positive emotions in relation to the work you need to do. By increasing the positive feelings you associate with a task, you'll be more likely to jump in on it. In fact, you want to make it so easy to start that it doesn't inconvenience you in the slightest and it's almost like you aren't doing anything at all. You may not be in a mood to do anything difficult, but something neutral might be possible.

Suppose you need to create a PowerPoint presentation of your company profile. To set a low threshold, decide to only work on just the titles of each slide, or even just pick a background design. Leave the actual details and content for later; it's not pertinent to your current threshold and goal of just getting started. Score an easy win and start to gain momentum that leads you away from the couch.

A low threshold doesn't only have to be with regard to the time commitment. It can also be in regard to the *quality* of what you're producing. Instead of trying to write five hundred words a day, try to write five hundred words of *crap*—lowering your standards will help you stop overthinking and simply get into action.

Creating a low threshold to get started touches upon one of the greatest obstacles—viewing a task as the larger end product. When something is so big and insurmountable, it feels pointless to do anything.

Thus, try to focus on the process rather than the product. While product pertains to the outcome of your efforts, process refers to the actions you take and the flow of time that passes as you work toward that outcome. The end goal will never change, but it's about how you view it.

If you've ever witnessed or heard how the Japanese conduct tea ceremonies—how every step of the ceremony has significance and is thus done with the utmost care and respect—you'll easily recognize what a focus on process rather than product looks like.

For the Japanese, tea ceremonies aren't done just so one can produce and fill their bellies with tea. Rather, the ceremonies are done for their own sake—the process itself has more significance than the product does. And when you focus on the process and dedicate your full attention to it, the product inevitably comes as a result of that process—the tea gets made and drank in the end.

Now, how does this relate to procrastination? When you need to do something, especially if it's a large task, it's easy to get overwhelmed by the pressure of having to deliver the product.

This pressure is usually enough for people to opt for procrastination instead of taking on that task. To avoid this, try to focus on the process of doing that task. What do you need to do in order to get the job done? Break things down into smaller tasks, then schedule these tasks to be done within chunks of time spread out over days or weeks. These smaller tasks are easier to swallow mentally, and the bite-sized portions relieve you of pressure by allowing you to focus just on one particular work block at a time, rather than allowing you to get intimidated by the idea of an overarching goal.

For example, suppose you need to devise a handbook intended for visitors who come by your company. The handbook is your product. Thinking about this product in its entirety—must include everything from company background, vision and mission, organizational chart, and safety reminders for visitors—can trigger overwhelming feelings of dread about having to undertake such a mammoth task.

So instead of focusing on the product (i.e., the entire handbook), focus on the process of creating that product section by section. Assign yourself only one section for a particular chunk of time—say, piecing together the organizational chart for this hour. Do the next section at another scheduled time, and so on, until you complete the entire thing.

Keep your eyes focused on what's in front of you and just complete your tasks. By focusing on a section-by-section approach, you get to ease into the process and feel that you're accomplishing things throughout instead of experiencing a sense of success only at the end of it.

Think of this strategy as similar to building a structure brick by brick. You'll be better motivated to start working and keep going when you know you just have a specific number of bricks to lay at a time, rather than expecting yourself to plop down a huge structure all at once.

Because you have no unrealistic expectations of yourself, you're also saved from having to feel an overwhelming amount of pressure to accomplish the impossible. You get to pace yourself well and don't feel guilty about "just laying ten bricks for the day" because you're well aware of the fact that those "ten bricks" constitute enough work that'll still allow you to achieve your goal on time.

Second, forgive yourself for procrastinating.

One way that you get overpowered by procrastination is by letting yourself think that your past procrastination slip-ups are irredeemable and that they have done such irreparable damage that you might as well give up on trying to remedy the situation altogether. You feel guilty and blame yourself for being too weak to fight off procrastination, so you get discouraged trying to do the task any longer.

For instance, you may think that because you've procrastinated on doing that research project for the past hour, any attempt to start researching now is already a lost cause, so you decide to spend the rest of the evening just procrastinating. When you forgive yourself, you stop thinking in terms of lost causes, move past wallowing in self-pity, and move to the next phase, which is action.

Instead of wallowing in that bottomless pit of self-blame and guilt, resolve to forgive yourself for procrastinating and pick up the motivation to start anew once you recognize you've slipped up. As associate psychology professor Michael Wohl found in a 2010 study, university freshmen who forgave themselves for putting off studying for the first exam procrastinated less on the next exam. Forgiving yourself for procrastinating thus decreases the likelihood of you later procrastinating on your tasks. Instead of being problem-focused ("I can't believe I have so much to do!"), become solution-focused ("What steps do I take now?").

Someone with the problem-oriented mindset obsesses on the problem itself. They wonder what went wrong. They get upset that it keeps happening. They seek blame and responsibility for the problem, and the only answer they have for the problem is to "avoid it." They are unable to move past their negative feelings regarding a problem or obstacle.

To come up with a solution in this mindset, determine what your existing conditions are now (Point A) and how you eventually want them to turn out (Point B). By getting a clear understanding of each point and the gap between them, you'll get a much better sense of what you need to do.

Think of the problem in terms of checklists. You could make a list of everything that's going wrong. Alternatively, you could make a list that describes potential solutions. Only one of these checklists is actionable. The only actions you can derive from a list of problems are complaining and fixating on failure. With a list of actions, you have options you can immediately pursue. Only the action list has real value.

Out of Sight, Out of Mind

Let's continue and look at other subtle but powerful shifts in perspective that can help us move out of the passive, stuck, and unproductive mindset that so often characterizes procrastination.

If we *know* procrastinating is bad for us, why do we still keep doing it? As previously discussed, biological explanations point to the roles of the lizard brain running wild with primitive drives and impulses and to the prefrontal cortex not being strong or skilled enough to get those drives and impulses under control.

But what about the psychological explanation for our proclivity for doing something that actually causes problems for us? What is it in our human psyche and cognitive processes that predisposes us to put off tasks until later, even when we know we should really be doing them now, and even when we know that we're harming ourselves as we do so?

You might be surprised to learn that this is an old problem that even the ancient philosophers chewed on (the Greeks called their version "akrasia"). According to business site Harvard Business Review, though, we can chalk it up to what is known as *omission bias*. Omission bias is a cognitive distortion by which we fail to see the consequences of *not* doing something.

While it's easy for us to envision the consequences of committing something bad, it's harder for us to imagine the costs of omission, i.e., the "opportunity costs" and what we lose in potential. This is because when we perform or witness an action, we are primed to anticipate an effect that arises out of that action. We wait to see what happens afterward. But when there's no tangible action, our minds find no reason to try to see how that might change things for us.

We tend to just go about our lives not even thinking of omission as possibly having effects, precisely because we think there wasn't an action to cause any effects in the first place. Essentially, out of sight, out of mind.

For instance, it tends to be easier for us to picture how frequently eating a load of greasy fast food meals is going to risk our heart health, but it's harder for us to recognize how *not* exercising can place us at the same health risk. While we may actively avoid those oily takeout meals in an attempt to maintain a healthy lifestyle, we aren't as likely to start an exercise regimen to support that same goal. It just doesn't have the same psychological impact.

Omission bias is often at play when we procrastinate on tasks. See, procrastination is essentially an omission—it's the phenomenon of *not* doing our intended tasks. Owing to our bias against considering the pros and cons of not doing things, we tend to feel less alarmed by our procrastination tendencies, because technically, since we're not doing anything, our minds take that to mean we can't possibly be doing anything wrong.

Our minds reason, *"How can we be doing anything wrong if we're literally not doing anything?"* Such is the brilliant "logic" of our mind: bending reason to support our procrastination habits so we get to continue reaping short-term pleasures while remaining blind to the negative impacts of our inaction.

So how do you get out of the rut that omission bias creates for you? The answer starts with awareness. Once you're better aware of the gravity of consequences attached to not doing a task, you'll also be more motivated to start doing that task. Recognize how omission bias tends to operate in your life, how it has sabotaged your motivation to work on tasks in the past, and how it's likely to affect your future decisions and actions.

Proactively magnifying the negative effects of omission bias on your life is a powerful way to confront it and a key strategy to transition from procrastination to productivity. There may not be any immediate negative effects, but as you start to think outward from yourself and into the future, more and more will materialize. More than simple awareness is needed from time to time.

For example, say you've been putting off your task of reviewing and updating your company's current policies and procedures on chemical disposal. If you aren't aware of your own omission bias, you'll likely feel as if you're not really doing anything wrong, because there's a current system in place that's working anyway. However, you're conveniently ignoring the negative impact that *not* doing that task might carry, including health risks for everyone in the community.

Continuing to employ outdated chemical disposal methods may be poisoning your neighborhood's water supply or hazarding the health of all company employees, including your own. But without proactively imagining these negative effects of inaction, you'll be less likely to feel the urge to act. To remedy the situation, reconsider the negative consequences of not doing the task at hand and use it to motivate yourself to get working.

Visualize Your Future Self

When we can consider what is unseen, when we pause to analyze our options and actions and think about the risks and potentials in our strategy, we are employing our higher intellectual functions, i.e., that part that will temper and moderate the lazy lizard brain.

Remember that the defining feature of procrastination isn't just the act of putting off tasks; it's the deliberate delaying of intended tasks, even while knowing full well that such delay will cause negative consequences in the future. Well, guess who suffers in that scenario? Procrastination isn't just about complacency or mere forgetfulness. It's more about hazarding the welfare of our future selves as we focus on gaining short-term pleasure at the cost of long-term benefits. And as we've seen with the omission bias, the problem is our mindset and where we're choosing to place our attention.

The solution is to occupy your higher mind and, essentially, force yourself to think about what you're not thinking about.

Psychologist Dr. Pychyl suggests that you "time travel."

Don't worry: this book hasn't taken a turn to sci-fi-ville. Time travel here pertains to the practice of projecting yourself into the future as a way to anticipate how good you'd feel if you finish a task and how bad you'd feel if you don't. Considering the future is something the lizard brain can't do, to its own detriment.

Vividly think about your future self and how they will feel. This strategy remedies the tendency to get so caught up in your present anxieties—or present pleasures—such that you fail to appreciate the relief and sense of fulfillment that comes once you accomplish a task and the horror that comes if you don't.

When you can associate immediate actions with longer-term consequences, suddenly you gain perspective on what you should or shouldn't be doing. Visualize your future and all the positive and negative consequences that arise from a small, immediate action. You can then make much more intelligent decisions. You can use your imagination. You can find new solutions.

For example, if you're not feeling motivated to work on a speech you've been asked to do, picture yourself already up on that podium in the heat of the moment. How would it go if you went into it well-prepared? What kind of applause would you receive, and how many accolades might you garner afterward? How satisfying is the feeling of a job well done, especially if it was a challenge?

On the other hand, how might you sound if you failed to prepare for it well enough? How red would your face be if you were stumbling for words, and how much brow sweat would accumulate? How might a poor performance change people's perceptions of you? Soak in that feeling of anxiety and panic.

Now you have a very clear picture of what's at stake. Picture the pains and the triumphs and use them as a mental boost. Admittedly, the pains will probably be more motivating, but that's okay. In small doses, pushing yourself using fear is a necessary evil.

Other scientists have supported this notion. Research into chronic procrastination has unearthed an interesting discovery on what sets apart chronic procrastinators from the rest. We each have a way of transporting our mind into the future—we do it whenever we set goals, plan, or bring up positive affirmations.

Through these activities, we're able to connect with our future selves and visualize how we're going to transition from our present situation to that future vision. For chronic procrastinators, though, that vision of their future selves tends to be blurry, more abstract, and impersonal.

They often feel an emotional disconnect between who they are at the present and who they'll become in the future. Thus, they have a harder time delaying gratification. As they are more strongly in tune with the desires of their present selves and don't feel connected enough with their future selves to care about their welfare, chronic procrastinators thus more readily give in to the lure of short-term pleasures.

Rather than sacrifice present comfort for future rewards, they choose to revel in what feels good now because their vision tends to be more limited to the immediate moment. This is what psychology professor Dr. Fuschia Sirois calls *temporal myopia* (more easily thought of as nearsightedness with regards to time)—a key quality that may largely underlie chronic procrastination.

To further clarify the phenomenon of how our perception of time can influence the way we make decisions, Hal Hershfield, a professor of marketing at UCLA's Anderson School of Management, conducted experiments. Using virtual reality, Hershfield had people interact with their future self.

The results of his experiments revealed that people who interacted with their future selves were more likely to be concerned about both their present and future selves, and they also tended to act favorably in consideration of their future selves. For instance, they were much more likely to put money in a fake, experiment-based retirement account for the benefit of the future self they interacted with.

What did Hershfield's studies show us? The better we're able to visualize and interact with our future self, the better we get at taking good care of it. This is because by visualizing and connecting with our future self, we feel the reality of the upcoming circumstances and recognize how the actions of our present self are bound to create a real impact on our future self.

By practicing visualization, we start to see how procrastinating now may be good for our present self but disastrous for our future self. As we empathize with the fate of our future self and the kind of life it will have to live through if we keep the habit of procrastination up (e.g., sleepless nights trying to get caught up with work, turning in haphazardly done output, having to deal with career failures), we begin to feel motivated to change our present ways to be more productive.

So the next time you're feeling drawn to procrastinate, think of your future self. Visualize every little step and reaction your future self would make in both situations. Getting a taste of the two alternate lives your future self might experience will increase your motivation to act toward realizing your success rather than the failure.

As you come to appreciate the beauty of a success scenario, visualize what the completed task looks like and trace your way back—that is, outline the specific tasks you need to perform to get to that vision of your future self proudly completing the task at hand and reaping its rewards.

Keeping your future self in mind will serve as a reminder both of the positive consequences of beating procrastination and of the negative impacts of failing to fight the urge to delay your intended tasks.

The If-Then Technique

The final technique dealing with your mindset is the *if-then technique.* This is also sometimes known as an *implementation intention*—in other words, making your intention easy to implement. The *if* portion corresponds to the cue, while the *then* portion corresponds to the routine.

If-then statements take the following form: if X happens, then I will do Y. That's it. This helps you avoid procrastination because you never deal with it in the heat of the moment. You make the decision beforehand. When actions are chained and given forethought, they tend to happen more often than not.

As a quick example, *if* it is 3:00 p.m. on Sunday, *then* you will call your mother. *If* it is 3:00 p.m., *then* you will drink two liters of water. *If* you have just taken a break, *then* you will take care of some chores. These are examples of when you use if-then to accomplish a specific goal—the first type of use. X can be whatever event, time, or occurrence you choose that happens on a daily basis, and Y is the specific action that you will take.

The if-then statement simply takes your desired goals out of the ether and ties them to concrete moments in your day. A goal to eat healthier or get started on work has a set prescription because it is tied to a daily occurrence that is unavoidable. Instead of generalities, you get a time and place for when to act.

It seems simplistic, and it is, but it has been shown that you are two to three times more likely to succeed if you use an if-then plan than if you don't. In one study, ninety-one percent of people who used an if-then plan stuck to an exercise program versus thirty-nine percent of non-planners. Peter Gollwitzer, the NYU psychologist who first articulated the power of if-then planning, recently reviewed results from ninety-four studies that used the technique and found significantly higher success rates for just about every goal you can think of, from using public transportation more frequently to avoiding stereotypical and prejudicial thoughts.

Let's say your significant other has been giving you a hard time about forgetting to text to inform them that you will be working late and not make dinner. So you make an if-then plan: if it is 6:00 p.m. and I'm at work, then I will text my significant other. Now the situation "6:00 p.m. at work" is wired in your brain directly to the action "text my sugar bear."

Then the situation or cue "6:00 p.m. at work" becomes highly activated. Below your awareness, your brain starts scanning the environment, searching for the situation in the "if" part of your plan. Once the "if" part of your plan happens, the "then" part follows *automatically*. You don't *have* to consciously monitor your goal, which means your plans get carried out even when you are preoccupied.

The best part is that by detecting situations and directing behavior without conscious effort, if-then plans are far less taxing and require less willpower than mere resolutions. They enable us to conserve our self-discipline for when it's really needed and compensate for it when we don't have enough. Armed with if-thens, you can tell your fickle friend willpower that this year, you really won't be needing him.

All of these methods help focus on the minute but powerful triggers that lead us into the personal infractions we're trying to eliminate, and they help defray the residual personal reactions that arise from forcing change in our lives. Best of all, they don't rely on sweeping or exhaustive changes to who we are—they make our brains and natural impulses work *for* us instead of going to sleep on the job.

Once again, deciding exactly how you'll react to circumstances regarding your goal creates a link in your brain between the situation or cue (if) and the behavior that should follow (then). And as we know, everything good that we want happens in our brain.

Learn to push the right psychological "buttons" to rid yourself of procrastination and become a more productive individual. As you master the art of repairing your mood, confronting your omission bias, and visualizing your future self, you'll have less and less trouble starting up. Yes, as a human being with your own set of drives and impulses, you may never get yourself to work as simply as you can turn a machine on.

Takeaways:
- We can work with our own psychology to deliberately activate a motivated and productive mindset in ourselves. This requires us to learn to take on different perspectives and challenge our underlying expectations and beliefs around the work we're doing.
- One common and self-sabotaging belief is that we need to delay action until we feel ready, motivated, or inspired. The truth is that this debilitates us, and that passion and energy are often the result of taking action, not the cause. Lower the threshold to starting and focus only on one section of the task at a time.

- Omission bias is the name we give to the tendency to ignore or forget the consequences of *not* doing something, resulting in opportunity costs. Failing to act has negative consequences, and if we bring awareness to what we're losing by procrastinating, we can realize how it's not really worth it. This entails deliberately thinking about what you are losing out on by "doing nothing."

- We can also use visualization to counter another of our lizard brain's blind spots—the future. If we ignore the future and focus on instant gratification only, we set ourselves up for failure; instead, we can "time travel" and vividly imagine ourselves in the future after taking certain actions. This allows us to make more informed, conscious and intelligent decisions about the consequences of our present behavior.

- Finally, the If-then technique is another way to work around psychological limitations. *If* represents the cue, and *then* represents the behavior that follows. By creating if-then rules and conditionals for yourself, you connect desired activities to concrete parts of the day, and makes them more likely to happen. This technique also cuts down on decision fatigue and trains habit and consistency. Simply framing your intentions this way has been proven to improve your chances of actually following through.

Chapter 4: Get Off Your Butt

"The only difference between success and failure is the ability to take action."

—Alexander Graham Bell

Do your mindset and attitude matter? Undoubtedly. But, it is not the *only* thing that matters. In fact, a theme we'll return to again and again in this book is that at the end of the day, there is only one thing that truly crosses you over from the land of potential and into the land of the actual: ACTION.

In this chapter, we'll look closely at the battleground on which the drama of procrastination plays out: the immediate moment. Of course, we know procrastination is the devil on our shoulders that suggests we will be totally fine if we push what we should do until another moment, then another, then another, and then a few more after the next four. You get the idea. You've been there before, in that moment, facing down the choice to run away or to knuckle down and act *right now*. No matter how motivated you might have felt before, crunch time arrives and the rubber hits the road. In this chapter, we'll look at ways to deal with procrastination not from a distance, but staring at it head on in the moment.

What is it that makes us want to say, "I'll get to it later!" in the hopes that it will disappear forever? Whatever it is, this chapter is aimed at just getting started as a way to break inertia.

The 40-70 Rule

Let's begin with something you might find a little counterintuitive: can you actually be too prepared? Is this causing you to procrastinate?

Former U.S. Secretary of State Colin Powell has a rule of thumb about coming to a point of action. He says that any time you face a hard choice, you should have no less than forty percent and no more than seventy percent of the information you need to make that decision. In that range, you have enough information to make an informed choice, but not so much intelligence that you lose your resolve and simply stay abreast of the situation.

If you have less than forty percent of the information you need, you're essentially shooting from the hip. You don't know quite enough to move forward and will probably make a lot of mistakes. Conversely, if you chase down more data until you get more than seventy percent of what you need (and it's unlikely that you'll truly need anything above this level), you could get overwhelmed and uncertain. The opportunity may have passed you by, and someone else may have beaten you by starting already.

This is the zone of procrastination—you want one hundred percent information, and although it's never possible, it's a zone of safety.

But in that sweet spot between forty and seventy percent, you have enough to go on and let your intuition guide your decisions. In the context of Colin Powell, this is where effective leaders are made: the people who have instincts that point in the right direction are who will lead their organizations to success. This is also where you should battle procrastination before it becomes too late. You should feel a certain amount of uncertainty or even lack of confidence—it's natural, and anything else is an unrealistic expectation. More often than not, what you are searching for will only be gained through *beginning*.

We can replace the word "information" with other motivators: forty to seventy percent of experience, forty to seventy percent reading or learning, forty to seventy percent confidence, or forty to seventy percent of planning. While we're taking action, we learn, gain confidence, and gain momentum.

When you try to achieve more than seventy percent information (or confidence, experience, etc.), your lack of speed can destroy your momentum or stem your interest, effectively meaning nothing's going to happen. There is a high likelihood of gaining nothing further from surpassing this threshold.

For example, let's say you're opening up a cocktail bar, which involves buying a lot of different types of liquor. You're going to wait until you're one hundred percent ready with your liquor before opening.

You can't expect to have absolutely all the liquor you will ever need when the doors are ready to open. It's impossible to be able to serve any drink that a customer orders.

So, applying this rule, you'd wait until you had at least forty percent of your available inventory prepared. This would establish momentum. Then, if you could get more than half of what you need, you'd be in pretty good shape to open. You might not be able to make absolutely every drink in the bartender's guide, but you'll have enough on hand to cover the staple drinks with a couple of variations. If you have around fifty to sixty percent inventory, you're more than ready. When the remaining inventory arrives, you'll already be in action and can just incorporate that new inventory into your offerings. If you waited until you had seventy percent or more inventory, you could find yourself stuck in neutral for longer than you wanted to be.

This way of thinking leads to more action than not. It constantly reminds you of what's ultimately important: acting. Waiting until you have forty percent of what you need to make a move isn't a way of staying inside your comfort zone—you're actively planning what you need to do to get out, which is just fine (as long as it's not over-planning).

Banish Excuses

As we've seen, people use excuses to postpone taking action and to procrastinate. Most excuses, however, are poppycock—invalid, rubbish, and rationalized. Excuses are our subconscious protecting us from our fears. It is your automatic pilot saying, "Danger! This might not go well! Let me save you!" And the solution that pilot offers is always to avoid action. That's all it comes down to: some part of you is choosing procrastination because, on some level, you believe it is an effective strategy to achieving your goals (and that goal is often to stay safe and comfortable).

Let's look at some common excuses people use to procrastinate.

Now is not the right time. We saw this in the previous chapter, and it's worth repeating since it's probably one of the most common. Related variations: _I can't do X until . . . I can't do X unless . . ._ True. There is never a perfect time for anything. There are mediocre times and terrible times, but rarely are there perfect times. Stop putting conditions around your ability to work. All you are doing is creating a psychological gatekeeper for yourself that is detrimental.

Timing is everything—that's actually not true. Timing just _is_. There is no good time for a crisis, but they happen anyway. When trying to be productive, rarely is there an obvious time that is better than another. It's just a lie we tell ourselves. There are always going to be obstacles to overcome and hassles to manage. In fact, ninety-nine percent of the time you want to do something, the timing will be mediocre, one percent of the timing will be truly terrible, and that's it. There should never be any expectations of having perfect timing.

When is the right time to travel? When is the right time to get married? When is the right time to have a child? When is the right time to quit? You know the answer to these questions.

For instance, there is never a perfect time to sell a house. The housing market is unpredictable, and various rates are subject to change overnight. You also don't know what bids you will receive and if anyone will even view your home. On the other hand, there are some objectively horrible times to sell a house, like when a main employer in town lays off fifty percent of its workforce and interest rates take a ten percent rise.

Many of us wish timing was something we had more control over, but the fact remains that we rarely get to choose when something happens to us. We do, however, get to choose when we take action. If you find yourself questioning this, the time to act has already arrived.

I don't know where to start. You do; the problem is that you think you need an entire plan before starting. People need to stop expecting to see a clear path through to the end before they even begin.

Here is the secret: you don't need to know where you'll will finish in order to start. The number one college major for students entering university in the U.S. is *undecided*. Most eighteen-year-olds are not able to articulate what they want to study that will lead to a lifelong career. However, we encourage young people to get to college soon after high school. "Don't wait too long. Don't get too many responsibilities." During the four (or five) years they are on campus, most students declare a major and start working toward a degree that will eventually lead to employment.

We think nothing of this process; however, so many times in adulthood people become paralyzed because they don't see a clear finish line. Doing something today with what you have today is the key. Stop researching, stop agonizing, stop wasting time, and start doing. Do what you can do right now at this very moment, and you can figure out the next steps after. You probably know your next steps, however small they may be.

The blank page or the blank screen is the writer's nightmare. It docs not matter if the writer is a middle schooler with a book report due or Stephen King. The blank page is terrifying. And yet, all who eventually produced something to fill that paper or screen had to stop reading the book, stop researching the topic, stop planning out the flow, and just start writing.

The first words written may not be any good. They may be terrible and need to be changed. But the writer cannot get there if they never write any words down. The way to start writing is simple: start writing. Focusing on the end product, a hardback with a glossy cover, isn't the goal at the beginning. A beginning is the goal. After you start, the rest will take care of itself because you will know what needs to be done to get you to the next step and then the one after that.

I'm not good enough. Shockingly, that just might be true. A person may really want to do something, but they might not be good enough. What is the answer to that dilemma? You can *become* good enough.

Sometimes the only way to get what you want is to shift into a growth mindset and start working. Make sure that this time next year, you know more than you know now and that your skills are better than they are now. If you are willing to take the first steps, what you need will follow.

When you feel like you are not good enough, you might need to reframe it just a bit to "I'm not good enough at this moment." After all, why would anyone have the expectation that they would be good enough at something without practice, work, and a significant amount of time? You simply cannot have the expectation of instant or even preemptive excellence. If you never start, you will never be good enough, and you will have prophesized your own future.

Learning a musical instrument is an illustrative example. When people say they aren't musical before picking up an instrument, it makes little sense, doesn't it? If learning to play the piano is your goal, then you can certainly make it happen. You would have to start back at that beginning middle C, but with lessons, practice, patience, and perseverance.

Anyone, including you, can learn to play the piano. Who knows? Perhaps you could eventually become a keyboard player for a Queen cover band. Just because you are not good enough now does not mean you cannot become good enough eventually.

Combating excuses is difficult because of our overwhelming need for self-protection. We may not even realize when we are using defense mechanisms to procrastinate, but chances are if you find yourself justifying a lack of action, it's a defense mechanism. Better productivity simply means removing that barrier to action.

Parkinson's Law

Parkinson's Law states that *work expands so as to fill the time available for its completion.* Whatever deadline you give yourself, big or small, that's how long you'll take to complete the work. If you give yourself a relaxed deadline, you avoid being disciplined; if you give yourself a tight deadline, you can draw on your self-discipline. So, this principle can be used in good or bad ways.

Bureaucrat Cyril Parkinson observed that as bureaucracies expanded, their efficiency decreased instead of increased. The more space and time people were given, the more they took—something that he realized was applicable to a wide range of other circumstances. The general form of the law became that increasing the size of something decreases its efficiency.

As it relates to focus and time, Parkinson found that simple tasks would be made increasingly more complex in order to fill the time allotted to their completion. Decreasing the available time for completing a task caused that task to become simpler and easier and completed in a timelier fashion.

Building on Parkinson's Law, a study of college students found that those who imposed strict deadlines on themselves for completing assignments consistently performed better than those who gave themselves an excessive amount of time and those who set no limits at all. Why?

The artificial limitations they had set for their work caused them to be far more efficient than their counterparts. They didn't spend a lot of time worrying about the assignments because they didn't give themselves the time to indulge. They got to work, finished the projects, and moved on. They also didn't have time to ruminate on what ultimately didn't matter—a very common type of subtle procrastination. They were able to subconsciously focus on only the elements that mattered to completing the assignment.

Very few people are ever going to require you or even ask you to work less. So if you want to be more productive and efficient, you'll have to avoid falling victim to Parkinson's Law by applying artificial limitations on the time you give yourself to complete tasks. By simply giving yourself time limits and deadlines for your work, you force yourself to focus on the crucial elements of the task. You don't make things more complex or difficult than they need to be just to fill the time.

For example, say that your supervisor gives you a spreadsheet and asks you to make a few charts from it by the end of the week. The task might take an hour, but after looking over the spreadsheet you notice that it's disorganized and difficult to read, so you start editing it. This takes an entire week, but the charts you were supposed to generate would only have taken an hour. If you had been given the deadline of one day, you would have simply focused on the charts and ignored everything that wasn't important. When we are given the space, as Parkinson's Law dictates, we expand our work to fill the time.

Set aggressive deadlines so that you are actually challenging yourself on a consistent basis, and you'll avoid this pitfall. A distant deadline also typically means a sustained level of background stress—push yourself to finish early and free your mind. Save your time by giving yourself less time.

The Energy Pyramid

When we put off our work, it's often because we have too little energy to do what needs to be done. When we experience our work as draining, we're too tired to focus, we're easily distracted, and we feel like we can't accomplish the job we've been assigned, what we're really experiencing are symptoms of poor energy management.

This is a bigger problem than we realize, because even more so than time, energy is a finite resource that we must protect on a daily basis. Nothing else you read in this book will make an iota of difference if you don't have the energy to pull it off.

Energy drains, and once it does, recharging is necessary. One great tool to understand energy management is the energy pyramid, an idea conceived by Jim Loehr and Tony Schwartz in *The Power of Full Engagement: Managing Energy, Not Time, is the Key to High Performance and Personal Renewal.*

The energy pyramid is a four-tiered pyramid with *physical energy* at its base, *emotional energy* above that, *mental energy* in the next layer, and *spiritual energy* at the top. Each of these plays an important role in building up or draining our energy, and each tier depends upon the tiers below to sustain itself. Understanding the interconnected nature of what goes into the energy we have for work allows us to take charge and create more for ourselves. Put another way, if you don't satisfy these levels of energy and engagement, it's unlikely that you will even be in a position to be able to focus and work, much less conquer procrastination.

To manage our energy, the pyramid points out that we must first notice and improve our levels of physical energy. Physical energy forms the basis for all the other tiers; it's the foundation upon which all our energy needs are built. To manage our physical energy, we mind our physical health. We eat healthy, get enough sleep, and exercise.

That may sound draining, and sometimes it is. After all, if you're not used to eating vegetables, indigestion will be the initial response to your newly healthy diet. But with time and persistence, eating well pays off with adjusted gut flora and an excess of energy. Exercise works the same way. At first, exercising feels draining, and we finish our routines exhausted. But after we've done it for a week or two, we start to feel energized when we've finished. What used to be difficult becomes easy, and when it does, it comes with a burst of fresh energy to apply to the rest of our lives.

Sleep, at least, is an activity that always feels good when we're doing it. While plenty of us wish we didn't need to sleep and could keep working without respite, it's a nonnegotiable fact of life that humans need rest. Without sleep, we yawn, have trouble focusing, and eventually fall asleep amidst our required activities. By contrast, when we put effort into getting our sleep, we're energized, ready for our day, able to focus, and unlikely to fall into an ill-timed slumber.

The best part about the physical foundation of the energy pyramid is that it's not an absolute scale. We don't have to become as athletic as teenagers, as health conscious as dieticians, or as well rested as Winnie the Pooh to benefit from healthy changes. All we have to do is find room for improvement, then improve. The benefits are almost immediate, and noticing and focusing on how much better minding our health makes us feel can motivate us to continue improving.

Once we start improving our physical health, we'll have the energy to consider the next level of the pyramid, emotional energy. Tending to our physical needs first is essential because our emotions depend upon our physical health. When we're too tired or hungry or malnourished to think clearly, we simply can't focus on emotional pursuits.

Emotions that don't result directly from our physiological state can help or hinder our ability to work, as well. Positive emotions like joy, anticipation, excitement, or even feeling challenged increase our engagement and our energy. By contrast, negative emotions like anxiety, frustration, sadness, anger, and bitterness crush us like heavy weights.

When we're overcome by these emotions, it's difficult to focus on our work and apply ourselves. But emotions aren't things we choose. Sometimes we're anxious when we know we'll be fine, and sometimes we're angry when we know we have no right to feel mad. Sometimes terrible things happen, and we feel sad or wronged; but even when negative emotions are justified, they don't help us learn, grow, and add value to the world.

The best weapon against these modern monsters is *reframing*. When you face a challenge you don't think you can overcome, don't lament the inevitably of failure, but think about how much you can learn and grow even if you lose—after all, it's exactly those sorts of failures that form the foundation of success. No one accomplishes everything on the first attempt; failure is what teaches us what to do differently to perform better in the future. A sense of being wronged and a base desire for revenge against the universe is one of the more common negative emotions that can be easily overcome by a shift in focus. The majority of what's happening in anyone's life is never bad.

Feeling good is essential to doing good. Focusing on those tiny gifts and cultivating gratitude goes a long way toward making us emotionally healthy. To feel good, we have to be willing to let go of negative emotions and be grateful for the positive aspects of all things. Happiness flows freely when we do our part, and when we're happy, we're both more energetic and better at finishing our tasks.

Mental energy is the third tier of the energy pyramid. For us to be mentally energetic, we must first be emotionally and physically energized; otherwise, our exhaustion or unhappiness will be too difficult to overcome. Mental energy relates to everything about our conscious thoughts and it allows us to be productive.

This tier asks us to take control of our thoughts. Instead of passively accepting the first thought that comes to mind, we can assess our thoughts and respond to them in order to consciously choose what we think. This will modify our outlook, allowing us to determine whether we're expecting the worst or anticipating great things.

When we make the right choices, our work is easier to handle; we can even be energized by a problem we encounter because it will feel more like a puzzle than a harbinger of our own destruction.

An important part of building mental energy is to go into tasks with optimism. When we go into things with a negative outlook, we presume we will fail. For example, children often won't try new foods because they "don't look" tasty. Often, if we can convince kids to try food despite their initial judgment, they won't like the taste, either. They'd already made up their mind that the food wasn't good, which is the reason they disliked it. But the opposite is also true; when kids look at food and think they might like it or when they're convinced to withhold judgment, they often enjoy new foods.

It's the same with adults and tasks we need to complete. When we go in excited to show what we can do, we often do a superb job; if we go in presuming we'll fail, it's often hard to produce any work at all. On top of that, we're drumming up fear from the previous tier while we tell ourselves it's not going to work.

Aside from optimism, several tools can get us in the right mental mindset. Self-talk, where we engage in dialogue with ourselves, can dismiss less helpful thoughts and give us truer narratives to believe. Internal pep talks can work, too.

Visualizing the completed project can give a sense of reality to the finished process, and meditation uses our minds to calm the tension we can retain physically and emotionally. Even managing our time better can come into play at this level of the energy pyramid, as our minds are what we use to schedule our time and assess how long tasks could and should take.

When we manage our time, guide our emotions, and make sure our thoughts are helping instead of hindering us, we'll have more energy and find it easier to face the tasks before us.

After our minds are managed, we face the peak of the pyramid, spiritual energy. This isn't a religious or spiritual tier; rather, it encourages us to understand our core values and to align our actions with those values. For example, a person who values helping people might do excellently in healthcare jobs but flounder horribly in sales jobs because their values are met in one career path but not in the other.

The spiritual tier is about finding purpose in our work, which is the best motivator that exists. Personal drive only happens when our actions are aligned with our core values. To do that, we must choose work that aligns with our values and get away from work that runs counter to what we consider important in life.

When we're doing what we feel is important, there is strong motivation to keep going and to be glad when we accomplish tasks. Aligning ourselves with our work is the strongest motivator that exists.

Physical, emotional, mental, and spiritual energy are all part of the first principle of energy management. When we attain everything the pyramid implies, we're certain to be bursting with energy, but we won't yet know how to direct and manage that energy effectively. In fact, we may be so enthusiastic about what we're doing that we risk burnout.

How do we avoid that? With the second principle: every time we use energy, we must also allow for its renewal. No one, no matter how much energy they have, can keep going at full bore forever. Rest is necessary, not just for our physical bodies, but also for our minds and hearts.

When we don't take a break from what we do, we eventually become stressed out and frustrated; these are negative emotions that are often accompanied by negative thoughts. Both will sap energy quickly.

To prevent this, we must disengage regularly so that our minds can heal. Overuse, even overuse of energy, leads to destruction of the resource that's being overused. Rest is what allows us to heal and grow stronger.

Contrasting with the second principle, the third principle of energy management reminds us that pushing past our limits is necessary for growth. We can't just sit idly, work consistently, and expect to improve. We must regularly challenge ourselves if we want to grow.

Dancers know this very well. Everyone shows up to their first class barely able to point their toes and unable to point their toes to the degree the teacher desires. But pushing allows muscles to grow stronger and the body to take new forms. Sometimes it takes years of persistent effort to reach our true goals, but the way to get there is always by setting up a challenge and getting closer and closer as our bodies, emotions, minds, and spirits allow.

Even nonphysical tasks require us to push ourselves into discomfort, as anyone who's done a bit of public speaking will know. Most are terrified the first few times, and often that terror is discernible to the audience. Speakers will shake, stutter, and go over sections of their speech multiple times. At first, it feels like it will never get better, but persistence makes the nervous speaker reassume their task despite the difficulty. Slowly, giving speeches becomes easier. Eventually, the truly persistent will discover that it's an enjoyable activity. But none of that is possible without feeling spurred on to succeed by the challenge of public speaking. At every level, we benefit from challenging ourselves and pushing ourselves into new and difficult circumstances.

The fourth, and final, principle of energy management states that we must create energy rituals to sustain full engagement. Despite the human ability to think and choose, most of our actions are based on habit. What we do, we usually don't think about. What we have to think about, we usually don't do, at least not for very long! That means that it's essential to transform energy-sustaining practices into persistent habits so that we don't have to remember or talk ourselves into helpful habits.

This will come as no surprise to anyone who's dieted in their life; generally speaking, any short-term starvation will lead to eating in our habitual way once we shed the weight. What happens next? The weight comes back, and we have to diet again. This is particularly damaging, as each time we fail to make a real and lasting change in our life, the return of the old actions and their consequences feels more and more inevitable. It's not inevitable, but avoiding the trap involves making real, permanent changes. The new way has to be sustainable; in short, it has to become a habit.

Two months of consistently performing any action will generally turn it into a habit, but until we reach that point, we have to put active effort into creating a new routine. We must make a choice not to eat certain foods, to go and exercise, or to drink a certain amount of water. But commitment and consistency are only needed at first. Eventually, thinking becomes unnecessary; we will have the rituals in place to be healthy, happy, and effective at our work.

Once we have the habits in place to maximize our productivity, and once we become used to challenging ourselves and resting to recharge our batteries, it becomes easier to direct our energy in any way we need. When we have enough energy, even the tasks we like to avoid become easy to face!

As you can see, the present moment can be positively cluttered with endless things getting in the way of taking focused, deliberate action. Whether you fail to act in the moment because you're overwhelmed at the size of the task, lacking energy, telling yourself some lame excuse, or wasting time "researching" before you act, the effect is the same—you delay action. We'll end this chapter as we started it:

there are millions of ways to stall and delay, but just one way to move forward. *Act*. Get ruthless with whatever is preventing that action, and you will master the present moment and make it all it can be.

Takeaways:

- Getting off your butt might be the very essence of conquering procrastination. Procrastination's mortal enemy is the immediate, present moment. So how do we seize that?

- Utilize the 40-70 rule as popularized by Colin Powell. This rule states the following: you only need between forty and seventy percent of the information, confidence, time, or preparation that you think you do. Anything else is just spinning your wheels and procrastinating, and one hundred percent of what you want is impossible from the starting line. So take action at seventy percent, at worst, because things won't improve by simply waiting longer.

- We are full of excuses for the protection of our ego. But of course, excuses are detrimental to your working spirit. It's important to realize that these excuses are largely fabrications. "Not right now"—there is never a perfect time. "I'm not good enough"—no, but you can become good enough. "I don't know where to start"—

start with what you can do right now, not only with an ultimate endpoint in mind.

- Pay attention to the energy pyramid. Energy, more than time and more than anything else, is what determines how much we get done. It is the scarcest resource because it drains on a daily basis. There are four aspects/levels to it, and each contributes to overall being able to focus and work: physical (no fatigue), emotional (no unhappiness), mental (no discouragement), and spiritual (no lack of purpose).

Chapter 5: Take the First Step

"Take the first step in faith. You don't have to see the whole staircase, just take the first step."

- Martin Luther King Jr.

For many of us, the act of focusing may not be the difficult part. Often, the difficult part is breaking through the inertia you've been accumulating and just getting started. You need to make that psychological leap from where you are into the unknown. This first step is often simultaneously the smallest and yet the hardest to take for this reason.

This is largely the same in any area or field. For instance, take the literal example of a car. For a car to start, a complex series of explosions have to occur in order to propel pistons into motion.

Only then can a car budge forward an inch. However, the second and third inches are far easier because momentum has already been built and inertia has been destroyed.

Unfortunately, we are in states of inertia and rest far more often than not. You know this place: the proverbial comfort zone. We struggle to take the first step, even if we might excel once we are in motion. In fact, we actively run from it through procrastination and avoidance. This is going to be the natural first step in creating relentless focus—because you can't create it if you can't get off your butt!

The great thing about a first step is that once it's taken, the ball is rolling. You're moving. It's easier to *keep* going than to *start* going. For those of us who end up cleaning our bathrooms and vacuuming our carpets when the time comes, this section is focused on those small tweaks that allow you to fearlessly and quickly take first steps toward anything.

Productive Mornings

A brilliant morning routine is your first and best tool for firing up your momentum each and every day. If you're someone who battles to get started with tasks in general, this is one area of life where you should put most of your focus.

Humans are creatures of habit and routine. In some order, you wake up, brush your teeth, sit on the porcelain throne, and get dressed. We all know that a wasted day often starts out on the wrong foot. Your morning sets the tone for your entire day, so what can you add to that morning routine that will jumpstart your day and let you focus on what you need to focus on?

We all know how easy it is to zone out in the morning and literally lose hours of your day by aimlessly browsing the internet. In the morning, because we're usually tired, it's too easy for the inertia of non-productivity to grab hold of us. Even if we're at work, sometimes it can take a couple hours to get into the swing of the day's tasks and goals. It might be after lunch before you're feeling ready to dive into something big.

This is clearly what we're trying to avoid. How can you make your mornings more productive, have greater output, and have less procrastination? Create a productive morning routine for yourself.

Your best productivity starts when you have clearly defined goals. Why not have those goals and a proper mindset in place the minute you wake up? After you buy into the morning productivity routine, you'll find that it will become instinct for you to do productive acts when you wake up, which will transition naturally into accomplishing bigger and bigger tasks.

Instead of clicking aimlessly on random websites, you will gradually begin to click over to your tasks and action items.

What's on this morning's productivity routine? It's a fixed checklist that is specific in its sequence.

- Wake up. Don't hit the snooze button. Don't you *dare*. We've covered this already.

- Check the daily checklist you created the night before. Reviewing your list will immediately let you know what's on the docket for the day so you can start thinking about how to tackle it. Let it simmer in the back of your mind subconsciously as you go about the rest of your morning routine. It's a good idea to write these down by hand so you don't have to encounter your tempting phone. Five minutes.

- NO SOCIAL MEDIA, NO EMAILS YET. Don't let these distractions cloud the priorities you carefully laid out the night before. These can also be incredibly distracting in the morning, so save what would otherwise be a wasted hour and leave the social media for a break later in the day. After all, there really isn't that much going on in the world that affects you on a day-to-day basis.

- Bathroom routines—cleaning, grooming, relieving. It is many people's first urge to do this, but I implore you to reconsider. If you can program yourself to hold off on these essentials until after you look at your daily checklist, then the daily checklist becomes essential as well. Ruminate on your checklist while you're going through this part of your routine. When you plant the seeds of your checklist in your mind earlier and intentionally don't act on them immediately, you accomplish two underrated things.

First, you get to think about it and know that you don't need to deal with them at that instant—a bit of the pleasant feeling of procrastination. Second, you eventually become eager to do it because you've been thinking about it; you actually grow a sense of anticipation about it. Ten minutes.

- Get started on something. It's key to do this before breakfast or coffee. You're seizing the anticipation you have built up from looking at your daily checklist. Start it before sitting down to breakfast. The reason? Because this just might keep your breakfast short and focused in anticipation of you getting back to your task. Be preoccupied during your breakfast or coffee. Often, this will drive you to keep working on it during breakfast as well. Hopefully you can isolate a couple of smaller tasks to start your day with a couple of easy, encouraging wins. Twenty minutes.

- Breakfast or coffee. Make sure you already know what you're going to prepare so you don't waste time trying to cobble something together from the contents of your fridge! It's a good idea to have the same thing for breakfast every morning so you don't need to devote any brainpower to it. Whatever the case, prepare beforehand so you don't have to make a decision in the morning. Instead, reserve your mind for being preoccupied with what you started earlier. Fifteen minutes.

- Check your emails. Yes, finally, check your emails and reply to the most urgent messages. I've waited until this point to include this because otherwise, you risk getting dangerously derailed from the other priorities you set the night before. You might have an urgent matter or two in there, but nothing that can't wait an hour. Sometimes we are beholden to others, but far less than we think. Just do what's necessary here, not a total overhaul of your inbox. Fifteen minutes.

- Re-evaluate your daily checklist after seeing if there are any urgent matters in your emails. Five minutes.

- Goof around. Indulge yourself a little bit to raise your mood for the upcoming productive day . . . but only after you've started the ball rolling on multiple fronts! This will naturally discourage you from goofing around, and you might even begin to skip this part of the routine. But still, this is necessary for most. Ten minutes.

As you can see, this morning routine will skyrocket your productivity by cutting the fat in your mornings and getting you right down to business. It sets the tone for the rest of your day.

When you are productive first thing in the morning, you'll end up producing a lot for the rest of the day. Don't let those opportunities pass you by. Mornings can be make-or-break in terms of your day's productivity, and which one they will be depends on whether you can seize the inherent momentum.

Break It Up

I've touched on this already, but another one of the keys to kicking your butt into gear is to make your gears very easy to get going. In other words, make your barrier to starting as small as possible by breaking your tasks down. We'll talk more about baby steps later in the book.

Case in point: Very few people want to go to work when it's raining cats and dogs outside. It's an enormous burden to overcome mentally. You'll get soaked, your shoes and socks will be puddles, and you'll freeze from head to toe. Oh, and your only umbrella is broken. It's such a burden that you don't even want to go through the motions of getting dressed and putting on your boots. You feel defeated before you even get started, so you never do.

A horrendously rainy day can feel just like trying to be productive. When we're faced with huge tasks that feel insurmountable, it's like looking through your window out at the rain. It's such an obstacle that everything feels impossible and pointless. We drag our feet, discourage ourselves, and bitterly complain the whole time.

A single huge task, such as "finish the two-hundred-page report," can certainly sound imposing, if not impossible. However, what if you were to break that monumental task up into tiny, individual, easy tasks that you can get to work on immediately? For example: preparing the template, finding the first three sources, creating a bibliography, outlining five hundred words of the first section, and so on.

Otherwise, you're starting each day staring at the task equivalent of a rainy day.

One of the biggest hurdles to productivity is looking at tasks as huge, inseparable boulders. It's intimidating and discouraging, and when those emotions arise, it's tough to avoid procrastinating because tackling a boulder is a tough sell. Unfortunately, this is a habit that plagues most people. They see only massive boulders and allow themselves to get emotionally thrown off-track.

Break up your big tasks into smaller tasks, and keep repeating until the tasks you have before you are so easy you can do them within a few minutes. Create small, manageable chunks that will be psychologically uplifting and acceptable, and you'll kick your production up instantly. Make your to-do list as long and articulated as possible with as many small tasks as you can list out.

Productivity is nothing without action, and action is much easier with something simple and easy to warm up with. Small steps can take you to the top of the hill and let you roll down the other side to seize momentum. They help you break the inertia that leads you to passivity and inaction.

When you can knock out any task in a matter of minutes, you create more confidence in yourself to tackle the bigger tasks. You feel more at ease, and your mind is imbued with the knowledge and confidence that you've already done quite a bit, so the rest won't be a problem.

Create small victories for yourself and think "manageable" and "immediate." Trying to wrap your mind around a boulder only freezes your mind up and creates analysis paralysis because you won't have any idea of where to start. When you look at the big stuff, your first thought is that it's too tough, impossible, or highly unpleasant. Small chunks are easy to visualize and imagine doing, which means half the battle is already won.

Let's take an example that we're all familiar with: working out. You want to lose one hundred pounds, a hefty goal. If you go into the gym every day thinking that you want to lose one hundred pounds, you're probably going to fail. It's a huge, enormous boulder of a goal. It might sound grand to proclaim, but in reality, it is going to be very hard to stick to because of how unbelievable it sounds.

You won't see much progress on a daily or even weekly basis, and you will understandably become discouraged. It's too much to face at once, like the rainy day from the beginning of the chapter.

What if you approached your weight loss goal by breaking it into small, manageable increments (goals) and tasks? This might look something like setting a reasonable weekly weight loss goal, creating daily goals of eating specific foods (and not eating others), and drinking water every hour. Eat one hundred fewer calories per meal. Go on walks after each meal.

If you hit your weekly weight loss goal and successfully drink water every hour, it is far easier to stay motivated and focused. Meeting your smaller weekly goal will give you a sense of accomplishment, whereas making an insignificant dent in your total goal (one hundred pounds) will only make you feel discouraged and as if the task ahead is too great to achieve.

These are small tasks that, if done consistently and correctly, will lead you to achieving your overall goal of losing one hundred pounds.

The emphasis here is on accomplishing small and immediate tasks and goals; these small victories will encourage and motivate you. Always seek to break your tasks up into smaller components, even if when the entire task is normal- or small-sized to begin with. Don't underestimate the power of small victories.

"Don't-Do" List

Sometimes when we're struggling to get started, it's because we can't choose what to fixate on. Too many things have the potential to command our focus, and sometimes we can't differentiate between what we should avoid and what actually deserves our attention (sounds a lot like decision fatigue, doesn't it?). Thus, the focus of this section is to make crystal clear what you should be getting started on.

Everyone knows the value of the to-do list. Even if you haven't read about it prior to this book, no doubt you've stumbled across tips elsewhere about using a to-do list to increase productivity.

My point is that everyone inherently *kind of* knows what they should be doing and when they need to do it by. The act of writing it down just helps remind them. This makes them more likely to do what they know they should be doing—more than if they didn't have such a list.

Granted, this is mostly common sense and not what you bought this book for. Well, here it is: not everyone knows what they *shouldn't* be doing. Along with your to-do list, it's equally important to make a *don't-do list*. Each day, we're faced with choosing tasks that will create the biggest impact for us, and there are many hidden obstacles.

Again, we all know the obvious evils to avoid when trying to upgrade productivity: social media, goofing around on the internet, watching *The Bachelorette* while trying to work, or learning to play the flute while reading.

It can be difficult to distinguish between real tasks and useless tasks, and it will require some hard thought on your part.

You need to fill your don't-do list with tasks that will sneakily steal your time and undermine your goals. These are tasks that are insignificant or a poor use of your time, tasks that don't help your bottom line, and tasks that have a serious case of diminishing returns the more you work on them.

If you continuously devote and waste your time on these tasks, your real priorities and goals will be left untouched. Here's what you should put on your *don't*-do list:

First, tasks that are priorities, but you can't do anything about them at present because of external circumstances.

These are tasks that are important in one or many ways, but are waiting for feedback from others, or for underlying tasks to be completed first. Put these on your don't-do list because there is literally nothing you can do about them!

Don't spend your mental energy thinking about them. They'll still be there when you hear back from those other people. Just note that you are waiting to hear back from someone else and the date on which you need to follow-up if you haven't heard back. Then push these out of your mind because they're on someone else's to-do list, not yours.

You can also temporarily push things off your plate by clarifying and asking questions of other people. This puts the ball in their court to act, and you can take that time to catch up on other matters.

Second are tasks that don't add value as far as your projects are concerned.

There are many small items that don't add to your bottom line, and often, these are trivial things—busywork. Can you delegate these, assign them to someone else, or even outsource them? Do they really require your time? In other words, are they *worth* your time? And will anyone but you notice the difference if you delegate the task to someone else? By taking on the task yourself, are you getting stuck in the weeds of perfectionism? These tasks are just wasted motion for the sake of motion and don't really matter in the big picture.

You should spend your time on big tasks that move entire projects forward and not myopic, trivial tasks. Often, these are useless tasks disguised as important ones, such as selecting the paint color for the bike shed in the parking lot of the nuclear power plant you are building.

Third, include tasks that are current and ongoing, but will not benefit from additional work or attention paid to them. These tasks suffer from diminishing returns.

These tasks are just a waste of energy because while they can still stand to improve (and is there anything that can't?), the amount of likely improvement will either not make a difference in the overall outcome or success, or will take a disproportionate amount of time and effort without making a significant dent.

For all intents and purposes, these tasks should be considered *done*. Don't waste your time on them, and don't fall into the trap of considering them a priority. Once you finish everything else on your plate, you can then evaluate how much time you want to devote to polishing something.

If the task is at ninety percent of the quality you need it to be, it's time to look around at what else needs your attention to bring it from zero to ninety percent. In other words, it's far more helpful to have three tasks completed at eighty percent quality versus one task at one hundred percent quality.

When you consciously avoid the items on your don't-do list, you keep yourself focused and streamlined. You don't waste energy or time, and your daily output will increase dramatically.

Why read a menu with food items that are unavailable? It's pointless. By preventing your energy level from being dissipated by those things that suck up your time and attention, a don't-do list enables you to take care of the important stuff first.

The fewer things that tug on your mind, the better—the kind of stress and anxiety they create only hampers or kills productivity. A don't-do list will free your mind from the burden of having too many things in the air because it eliminates most of those things! You can focus on the balls that are still in flight and steadily knock each one out.

Reward Yourself

I'm always amazed when I watch videos of dogs that can perform countless tricks.

How were their owners able to train them so effectively? Are dogs smarter than we think? Are they truly man's best friend? Yes and no. Their owners reward them with enough treats to make them fat. They bribe them with rewards that motivate them into action.

A dog will bend over backward, crawl through mud, leap through hoops, walk on two legs, do flips, and run obstacle courses if you make it clear you will be rewarding them properly afterward. Dogs become highly motivated and focused when they know something they want is at stake. It's as simple as that.

Imagine a rabbit with a carrot tied in front of him. The rabbit can't reach the carrot, but he keeps running faster and faster to get a bite of his favorite food.

We're not much different from animals. We function and focus far better if we have a clear goal and reward to work for. For the most part, if we choose our reward intelligently enough, it can lure us into action much sooner than we would even prefer, or be ready for. Just picture when you're exhausted and sleep-deprived but hear the familiar jingle of the ice cream truck growing louder. You might just draw yourself up and outside. Rewards get results.

Humans are creatures of incentives, and this is undeniable when we look at our daily actions. Everything we have and do is a reflection of the incentives we have and the reward we work toward. Whether our incentive is food, sex, social status, or money, we are driven by a perceived benefit or reward.

Knowing this, we can boost our daily productivity and spring into action by setting rewards for ourselves to keep us focused. If we do it properly, we can program ourselves to achieve amazing levels of productivity with simple rewards.

The first step is to define the rewards that will actually motivate you into action. You can also frame them as punishments. If you don't finish the task at hand, will you:

• Not get a snack?

- Not book your trip to Italy?
- Not get Chinese for dinner?
- Not hang out with that cutie tonight?
- Not buy that shirt for yourself?

For our purposes of getting started, we want to pair getting into action with something correspondingly quick and instant as a reward. This means we're probably looking at mostly short-term rewards, like rewarding yourself with chocolate the way a dog gets a treat for a trick.

This may not work for everyone, but the way that worked for me was literally stockpiling bags of chocolates so I could reward myself every time I had to use my willpower to get started and into action. I had them on-hand for a couple of weeks, and two patterns began to emerge.

First, it motivated me to action because I knew there was something pleasurable after engaging in the unpleasurable. This was predictable. Second, I actually began to associate the process and act of getting started with . . . pleasure. Just like Pavlov and his dog, I had become the dog who was able to create a positive association with breaking through my inertia, despite it being an innately uncomfortable act. I was able to condition myself. This may not occur with everyone, but it's certainly a possibility, given that our drives don't work much differently than a dog's.

Rewards can also come in the long-term form; they may not be so tangibly motivating and impactful, but they can push people into action because they begin to understand what's at stake.

For instance, put a picture of Italy or Hawaii up right by your desk so you are constantly reminded of what you're working toward and can positively motivate yourself, knowing you will only buy your plane tickets if you hit certain milestones you set. When you associate putting in the necessary amount of work with your reward, you take away the stigma of tedious work and slowly associate it with a happy ending.

When you use immediate, short-term goals in conjunction with overarching, long-term goals, you'll find more reasons than not to jump into action. Sometimes we just need a reminder to nudge us to take that first step.

There's a reason they call it work. I don't care whether you are a lawyer, a doctor, an accountant, or a dog trainer, certain parts of every job and task are a drag. When you use the power of conditioning yourself through rewards, you short-circuit this negative association, and the work becomes a means to a desired end.

In the end, it all boils down to what motivates you and having a clear view of what you're putting in all your work for. If you don't know what you're working for, then why would you work hard at all? It's like working at a job where you get the same compensation regardless of how hard you work. You go through the motions without direction or interest.

If your effort isn't tied to something that keeps you motivated, then why make an effort at all?

Takeaways:

- Focus is tough, but the toughest part about focus is simply getting started. It's because we all have to deal with a certain amount of inertia to begin our days. Getting into motion from a standstill takes energy, but there are ways to short-circuit the process for yourself.
- First, take note of Newton's law of momentum. This states that when an object is in motion, it tends to stay in motion, and when an object is at rest, it tends to stay at rest. How can you be an object that stays in motion? It starts with how you wake up,

begin your day, and don't allow time for inertia to set in.

- Productive mornings go hand in hand with Newton's law. When you can create a galvanizing and energizing morning routine for yourself, you can set the tone you want for the rest of the day. The morning routine that is recommended leaves little to no room for decisions or thought, and depends on planting the seeds of your tasks so you grow anticipation toward them.

- Getting started is easier when you have something small and easy in front of you. After all, it is easier to take a single step versus climb a mountain, even though they both have the same end goal. Therefore, break all of your tasks into smaller subtasks, and then do it again. This psychologically makes it easy for you to get started and take action.

- We all know what we should do, roughly speaking. But it's those things that we shouldn't do that sometimes keep us from getting started. We should avoid the sneaky tasks that are secret wastes of time. This should all be encapsulated in a "don't-do" list, where you make sure to note things to ignore and not pay attention to because they would distract you from what actually matters.

- Finally, motivate yourself into action with rewards. Make sure to use short-term rewards to instantly provide yourself with pleasure after getting started. Pair this with long-term goals that keep you motivated on a deeper level. Both of these have the pleasant side effect of taking the stigma away from your work and creating a positive and happy association with it.

Chapter 6: Create and Seize Momentum

"Success is like a snowball . . . it takes momentum to build and the more you roll in the right direction, the bigger it gets."

- Steve Ferrante

Now that you've gotten off your butt and into action, everything will be smooth sailing, right?

Yes, in a world where we are all millionaires and ride tigers as our main form of transportation. In other words, no; while just getting started is the most difficult part, that doesn't mean it's the *only* part of gaining focus and launching into productivity.

Once you've gotten started, you're in a delicate stage where you have to protect your focus to make sure that you properly create momentum for yourself. Otherwise, you'll sink back to inaction—and if you thought getting into motion the first time was difficult, the second time will prove to be near-impossible.

To borrow from another field, think about how daunting and difficult it is to walk up to an attractive member of the opposite sex and introduce yourself. Yet, it is the words directly after the introduction that matter the most and determine how the interaction will ultimately go, despite the fact that the introduction was more difficult. This section is focused on how to pick up steam and turn into a focused productivity machine.

Kill Perfectionism

Have you ever heard the term "don't let the perfect be the enemy of the good"? Perfectionism is one of the most important beasts you'll have to slay to create and maintain momentum. Perfection taken to an extreme degree has another name: obsessive-compulsive disorder (OCD).

Yes, your perfectionism can be similarly unhealthy and damaging to your focus and productivity.

If you have to lock and unlock your doors five times before you can leave your house, it's no different than editing a document for the fifth and unnecessary time. It prevents you from doing what you want in a timely manner, all in the name of making sure something is picture perfect. When we look at someone with OCD who's struggling with their tendencies, all we see is unnecessary motion for no real reason. Perfectionism in regard to your work will similarly keep you paralyzed. Both mindsets are driven by the (faulty) belief, "If only I do XYZ, then everything will finally be ok."

Perfectionism may seem like a good thing, but it's nothing more than an obstacle. Usually, wanting things to be perfect only means they are never actually finished. Defeating your perfectionist tendencies is one of the best things you can do to remain in motion and create momentum. This is because, almost universally, what's more important is what you actually follow through with something, not that something is flawless. It's far better to bring one hundred cookies to a bake sale than twenty perfectly iced cookies. And it's *far, far* better to perform three surgeries to adequate completion rather than perform one surgery to precise perfection. Perfection is not what makes the world go 'round.

In every area of life, perfection is not expected, and there are always buffers for a margin of error. Did you know that in preserved goods, there is an acceptable number of insects that might be mixed in? Sometimes disgustingly, we can't create perfection, and rarely does it ever make a difference.

In your personal life, because everyone makes mistakes of their own, a lack of perfection is almost always excusable. Everyone knows they make mistakes too, and they are in no position to judge you for something that isn't perfect. Everyone hits their own snags from time to time.

That's the first realization you must have to destroy perfectionism. Knowing that people accept imperfection is a big part of the mindset that will smash through your inertia and help you take your first steps. Your internal standards may be high, and you may be your own harshest critic, but the rest of the world does not operate on that rubric. It doesn't benefit anyone else in any tangible way, and it keeps you in a prison of your own making. Who are your perfectionist tendencies really serving? Only you, your fears, and your insecurities. That leads to the second realization.

The second realization is that perfectionist tendencies typically manifest to protect ego and pride—to make sure you are as rejection-proof as possible and to prevent a hit to your self-esteem.

For the most part, perfectionists are not necessarily driven by a need for excellence— they are really people who are petrified by judgment. They feel that any error on their part will reflect poorly on them as a whole, and people will cast judgment on their intellect or character. Thus, they leave as little to chance as possible by *perfecting* it.

To illustrate, think of the last time you praised an artistic friend's painting. Imagine that they were highly reluctant to show it to you because they felt that they drew a hand poorly. You surely can't tell, because to you the painted hand looks perfectly hand-like. You couldn't tell the difference between what you were seeing in the painting and your friend's standard of perfection. It made no difference to you whatsoever.

However, to your friend, they saw every little mistake and assumed that everyone else could as well. They fixated on the negative judgments the hand would create about them as a person, and thus kept working on the hand to the detriment of finishing the actual painting.

Your output is severely hampered when you waste time trying to *"get everything right."* Instead of producing fully, which the job or social situation might call for, you'll only produce a tiny fraction of what was expected or requested.

Often, this tiny fraction is useless by itself, so you have just left a job incomplete by giving in to your perfectionist tendencies. What good are five perfectly decorated cupcakes when you were supposed to bring twenty? Who wins in that situation? Certainly not the fifteen people who didn't get a cupcake, with or without sprinkles! And certainly not you.

Perfectionism slows you down. By always looking back and double- and triple-checking your work, you are going to be moving at a snail's pace. At best, you produce a mere portion of what you should, and at worst, you are completely paralyzed by "analysis paralysis" and produce absolutely nothing.

Let's be clear that minimum standards do exist. You can't expect to succeed with low-quality writing, for example, but a cost-benefit analysis must often be done to see what the optimal pairing of standards and speed is.

Perfectionism also destroys momentum, which is an *everyday superpower* that should be leveraged for maximum productivity and output. When you can't let go of your perfectionism, you bring your momentum to a screeching halt. And it takes a tremendous amount of energy to get it going again.

In this sense, perfectionism is procrastination because it allows you to avoid future steps. Instead of forging forward, you might always be looking over your shoulder.

Being "*in the zone*" is the sense of momentum, and that's almost certainly a result of letting go of perfectionism. It's when ideas are flowing from your brain to your hands or your keyboard and you aren't even thinking—you are acting. Not everything you're doing is going to be perfect in that zone, but it doesn't matter, because you just need to keep translating your thoughts into work or words.

Staying in perfectionist mode is incredibly inefficient. By definition, you are overly focused on getting every little detail correct. This means you're probably focusing on the *wrong* details while larger issues are lurking and waiting for your attention. It's a very easy trap to fall into, and even easier to get blindsided by.

It's not an easy thing to let go of, but attempt to focus on maximizing your output and on the bigger picture—because that's the real issue with perfectionists. They get caught up in the trees and lose sight of the forest, where the forest is the big picture goal they are working toward. Just realize there are diminishing returns on perfection while the big picture goal will still be sitting there, waiting.

First things first: Finish what you need, then invest more time in quality and performance. This leads directly to the next point.

Edit Later

There are a lot of sayings about writers and their profession.

The road to hell is paved with works-in-progress.

It ain't what you write, it's how you write it.

We are all apprentices in a craft where no one ever becomes a master.

And finally, my favorite:

Write drunk, edit sober.

But my second favorite, and the focus of this point, is this one:

Write first, edit later.

The overarching message is that you should finish everything you're writing (or doing, whatever your task may be) before you double-check and spend time editing and revising it. Don't become distracted by backtracking and killing your momentum. Keep moving forward until you finish. This doesn't only apply to writers, though writing and writers are a helpful illustration.

If you're a writer and you try to make every word choice and phrase perfect, you'll probably be writing at the snail's pace of one page a day. But guess what? Your perfect prose isn't the reason people will be compelled to buy your book. And moreover, there *won't be a book to buy* if you write so slowly, get mired in the details, and don't ever complete the manuscript.

So what's the point? *Do first, edit later.* This is a tactic that will skyrocket your productivity and momentum because it encourages you to push forward and get everything you can onto the page before getting bogged down by small details (and before some of your best ideas slip away while you're focusing on perfecting a sentence). Stay on target with the big picture goal and leave the details for when you have extra time.

It also encourages the maxim of *do first, think later*, which you will benefit from as well. Stop thinking and plotting before you put pen to paper and simply start writing. You'll get into the swing of it when you start doing it and find your momentum building. For writers, this means to start typing whatever comes to mind and let it eventually get around to what you originally intended to write about. You'll have more material to play with in the end, anyway.

The simple truth with most tasks in our daily life is that having all of *something* is far more important than having seventy-five percent of something that has been edited to perfection. Having an entire task, batch, or paper done is always the primary goal. Don't lose sight of that by spending time tightening up your work before you have everything you need. Completion is the goal.

Too many people mistake a well-edited task for productivity.

Here's a dose of reality: that's not what you're paid to do. You're getting paid for how much work you complete. A completed checklist has far more value than a well-edited fraction of that list.

The overarching principle behind this productivity tip is that you need to take action *now* and focus on reflection later when you have the luxury of time. You are in a race against the clock, whether you realize it or not. Capitalize on the momentum you have, finish what you have to finish, and *then* reflect on what you've done when you can look at all of it. This is where you can edit and polish. What's important is that you get everything out of the way and taken care of before you start tightening things up and perfecting them. That's what you do when you've completed your task.

If you're so focused on whipping everything into shape, it will take you a very long time to produce very little work. The world rewards productivity and results, not the effort or the process. There are no prizes for "almost" or second place.

I would even go so far as to say that output and productivity comes first and quality comes second. I'm not saying you should abandon the idea of producing quality work. However, you should put things in proper perspective and understand that *producing* comes first.

No book (task) = no money (payoff), no matter how beautiful your prose and vocabulary are.

Within the details, there are those that matter and those that simply do not. Sometimes you will get your best results by ignoring some details that aren't significant and just focusing on seeing through bigger tasks to completion.

Ship things out. Take care of business. Get it done. Make it so. Later, once you've finished what you need to finish, you can come back and increase the overall quality of the tasks you have completed. Momentum will come.

Batch Tasks

Henry Ford, founder of Ford Motor Company, got a lot of things right about cars. He had a few competitors back in the day, but a primary reason those names are essentially lost in time is because he was also the creator of the *factory assembly line.*

On a factory assembly line, workers focus on one task at a time.

This streamlines a process and makes it far more efficient than having a single worker see a project through from start to finish, switching between multiple tasks. It allows workers to specialize and perfect their task, which cuts down on errors and makes troubleshooting far easier. Workers didn't have to do more thinking than was necessary for the task at hand. For Ford, this made his automobile production efficiency and output shoot through the roof and dominate the market.

That, in essence, is what *batching* can do for you. It allows you to keep momentum instead of switching from task to task, interrupting your train of thought and having to start over constantly.

Batching is when you group similar tasks together to complete them all at once, or closely following each other. Ford's assembly line was essentially one hundred percent batching because his workers only performed one task incredibly efficiently.

Let's take a common example we can all relate to—checking your email inbox.

If you have any sort of online presence or job, you probably have a steady stream of emails trickling (or gushing) into your inbox every hour. Constantly checking your email is an extremely inefficient use of time. It interrupts other tasks and scatters your focus whenever you receive a new email. Many of us drop what we're doing to take care of something from an email. Then we have to start the original task over again because our flow and momentum has been interrupted.

Batching emails will considerably improve your productivity. An example of this would be to only check your emails at the top of every two hours and purposely ignore or block your inbox notifications. At first it might be difficult, but limiting how often you check email in this way allows you to focus on your tasks without constantly being distracted and having to re-acclimate yourself.

Perhaps more importantly, it teaches the lesson that saying "no" to some tasks is just as important as saying "yes" to the correct ones. Batching teaches the art of purposeful, deliberate ignorance so you can focus on other tasks. Imagine using this in conjunction with a "don't-do" list.

Switching from task to task is a large mental burden because you are stopping and starting from zero numerous times throughout the day. It takes energy to switch from task to task, and there are usually a few minutes wasted on regaining your bearings and figuring out the status of the task you were working on. Of course, these kinds of interruptions only lead to achieving just a portion of what you can and want to.

In the example of checking your emails, batching allows you to stay in a mindset of reading and composing emails with all its associated skills, tasks, and reminders. Email catch-up is a distinctly different mode than designing a new graphic for an advertising campaign.

What else can you batch? You can schedule all your meetings for one afternoon so you will have a free, uninterrupted morning to work. You can plan to do everything that requires computer access in the morning, and even batch parts of tasks such as those which require you to make phone calls. Just categorize your tasks and put everything similar together to maintain better focus and momentum.

You can also batch your *distractions*.

This isn't to distract and amuse yourself more efficiently. It's to make sure that you are conserving your energy and allowing your focused time to be exactly that—focused.

How can you batch distractions? For example, if you're burned out on a particular task, you might want to take a little social media break. By all means, take it! However, allot just a bit more time to check *all* of your accounts—ESPN, Refinery29, and whatever other distractions you occupy yourself with. Grab a new cup of coffee, take a brisk walk around the office, and say hello to your neighbor.

Get it all out of your system so that when you're back to work, you can have a solid and fixed block of time in which to focus. After all, if there is nothing new on your Facebook page, you will probably feel less compelled to check it. Once you knock yourself out doing all these distracting activities within the allotted time, you can switch to productive work for the rest of your hour. What's important is that you are taking a *planned* break versus an *unplanned* break.

Some have referred to this as the *Pomodoro Technique.* A Pomodoro is a thirty-minute block of time.

Twenty-five minutes of that time will be allotted to focused, hard work, while the remaining five minutes will be a break. Once you complete four Pomodoros, you are allotted a twenty-minute break. It works the same way as batching distractions, and it keeps you focused because you know you will have a reward distraction at the end of the work period. It might even drive you to finish as much as possible before your break.

The more you divide your attention among different activities, the less focused you'll be. When you begin doing something similar to the previous activity, you'll find it's much easier to get going because your mind is already geared toward doing a certain kind of task. Do all the similar tasks together, one after the other, and then move on to the next batch of similar or related activities. Effective batching can skyrocket your productivity no matter the context.

One of the biggest benefits of batching is that it prevents multitasking. Speaking of which . . .

Single-tasking

Who would be great at multitasking? An octopus with two heads. As in, to multitask effectively, one literally needs two brains and eight hands. Guess how many brains and hands we are short? It's just not within human capability to multitask effectively, no matter what you think or have been told.

Multitasking is a big, fat lie. You simply can't do more than one thing efficiently at a time, so don't try to split your minutes in different directions. You can either do one thing well, or you can do three things very poorly. Unfortunately, too many people believe in it, overestimate themselves, and suffer lousy productivity as a result.

The main reason multitasking is so appealing to so many people is that they have inflated views of their capabilities. Most people believe they're good at many things, including the mental clarity to constantly switch between tasks from minute to minute. There's a sense of denial regarding the need for setting time aside and truly focusing.

In reality, it's like speed dating—you only get to know each task a little bit, and you don't really have enough information to make good judgment calls. There is no sense of familiarity with the time you're given and you end up with similarly ineffectual results. Everyone thinks they can do it, but there is a big difference between watching television while eating a sandwich and completing two tasks which require thought and effort at once. No one can do it well, even if they think they can, and trying to do it at all will only make you lose focus and end up performing worse at everything.

Let's take Bob. Bob is on the phone, on his tablet, and on a computer. He gets an email that seems urgent, so he starts to answer it while he's still talking on the phone. He completely loses track of the phone conversation, and the report he pulled up on his computer will have to be completely re-read to be understood. It only took one call or email to completely throw Bob off-track and for all of the things he was juggling to fall out of the air and land on his head.

By multitasking, the only thing that you will achieve is that you will end up continually distracting yourself, because your mind is focused on too many things to process them all equally and efficiently. According to a study in the *New York Times*, it can take up to twenty-five minutes to regain focus after being distracted. That's twenty-five minutes you will waste trying to find your place and get into the right mindset again.

In 2009, Sophie Leroy published a paper that was aptly titled "Why is it So Hard to Do My Work?" In it, she explained an effect that she called "attention residue."

Leroy noted that other researchers had studied the effect of multitasking on performance, but that in the modern work environment, once you reached a high enough level, it was more common to find people working on multiple projects sequentially. "Going from one meeting to the next, starting to work on one project and soon after having to transition to another is just part of life in organizations," Leroy explains.

This is essentially the modern version of multitasking—working on projects in short bursts and switching between them, not necessarily doing them all at once. People may not actually be working on multiple tasks at the same time, but it's nearly as bad to keep switching between them in relatively quick succession. For all intents and purposes, this is modern multitasking.

The problem identified by this research is that you cannot switch seamlessly between tasks without a delay of sorts. When you switch from Task A to Task B, your attention doesn't immediately follow—a residue of your attention remains stuck thinking about the original task. This becomes worse, and the residue becomes especially "thick" if your work on Task A was unbounded and of low intensity before you switched, but even if you finish Task A before moving on, your attention remains divided for a while.

Leroy's tests forced people to switch between different tasks in a laboratory setting. In one of these experiments, she assigned the subjects a set of word puzzles to work on. In one of the trials, she would interrupt their work and force them to move on to a new and challenging task—for example, reading resumes and making hypothetical hiring decisions. In other trials, she let the subjects finish the puzzles before giving them the next task.

While the participants were switching between puzzling and hiring, Leroy would play a quick lexical decision game. This was so she could quantify the amount of leftover residue from the first task. The results were clear: "People experiencing attention residue after switching tasks are likely to demonstrate poor performance on that next task," and the more intense the residue, the worse the performance.

This doesn't seem too far of a stretch when you think about it. We've all experienced that frantic moment when we're doing too many things at once and suddenly find ourselves unable to do any at all. How can you concentrate on any task if you keep switching back and forth between two or more different things? You'll likely be stuck simply trying to make sense of everything and organize it so you can understand it. It will only force you to waste time trying to catch up to where you were instead of pushing forward. You'll take one step forward, but two steps back each time you try.

Multitasking may seem to be the best of both worlds, but when you're in situations where there are multiple sources of information coming from the external world or emerging from memory, you cannot filter out what is irrelevant to your current goal. This failure to filter means that you are slowed down by irrelevant information and will struggle to complete a task without distractions. It is much easier to focus on one thing at once, without letting distractions interfere, than to try doing several things at a time and overloading your brain with too much information.

There might be certain ways you can multitask one percent more effectively, but the overall lesson is just to avoid it whenever possible. The answer is in the name of the point: single-tasking. What does this mean?

To set everything else aside and not check, monitor, email, or even touch anything other than the current task you are working on. It requires singular focus and the purposeful and intentional tuning out of everything else. Switch off your notifications and ditch your phone. If you must be on your computer, keep only one browser tab or program open at a time. Put yourself into a vacuum; if you grow bored or want to procrastinate, there's only one thing for you to do to exit the vacuum.

A lot of single-tasking is about consciously avoiding distractions that seem small and harmless. The biggest culprits? Your electronic devices. Ignore them when possible. Keep a spotless workspace so your eye doesn't catch something that needs cleaning or adjusting. Ideally, single-tasking reduces your environment to a blank room because you shouldn't pay attention to any of it. Out of sight, out of mind.

Attempt to pay attention to when you are being interrupted or subtly switching between tasks. This is hard to catch at first and will require you to make conscious decisions against your instincts.

Something that will be very hard to resist is the compulsion to tell yourself that you must act on something immediately and interrupt your task. However, don't confuse urgent with important. Matters and people alike all want to masquerade as important.

To combat this urge, set aside a notebook to take notes for ideas that will inevitably spring to mind regarding other tasks. Call this your *distraction list*. Just jot them down quickly and return to your primary goal. Whatever they're about, whether it's something that needs to be taken care, or something new and creative that pops into your head, take note, but don't act on them right when they come. Don't chase random thoughts, which are the equivalent of shiny objects.

Some of these might make their way into your to-do list, but most will probably end up on the "don't-do" list. You can address them after your single-tasking period is over, and you won't have forgotten anything. It will keep your mind focused on one single task while setting you up for future success.

Get in the habit of taking notes in general—this simple act frees up your brain for the present moment and doesn't let the future or the past interfere. Great ideas come in a flash and are gone the next second.

A big part of focus is organizing your thoughts and ideas so you can remember them and efficiently implement them at a later time. If you fail to capture your ideas at the moment they present themselves, chances are great you will forget them and lose out on the potential flood of increased productivity.

Our memories are pretty unreliable; in fact, studies show that eyewitness reports from memory are a terrible source of evidence in criminal trials.

Write everything down, even if you think it's not going to be important. Chances are what you write down will be a thread that leads to another thread that may just lead to the answer you have been seeking for weeks. Maximize your focus by keeping yourself rooted in the present, but also set yourself up for future success through your writings.

When you're in the thick of a busy day, your mind doesn't turn off. Keep a running log of everything you write down with you at all times. You might be surprised at the small things that used to fall through the cracks in your life. It might be as simple as remembering to buy more milk, or as important as a key creative idea that may generate thousands of dollars for you.

The solutions to your problems can come to you in an instant. It would be a shame if you're not properly equipped to record these solutions. There's literally no cost to you—just the effort involved in cultivating a habit that *all* of history's greatest thinkers have practiced and excelled at.

Distraction Blackouts

In our quest to break out of procrastination loops and start being more productive, we have one more tool up our sleeves to protect and maintain the momentum we've gathered. It comes down to finding little pockets completely free of distraction. If you've ever lost your Wi-Fi connection while working, you know it was one of the most productive days of your life.

Without Wi-Fi, you couldn't check Facebook, Twitter, ESPN, Snapchat, Reddit, Instagram— you couldn't even watch Netflix! In other words, you couldn't access any of your most beloved distractions, and when the boredom set in, you actually had no choice but to focus on what you wanted to avoid.

You probably also completed it in record time. When we're faced with the choice of sitting and doing nothing for hours or focusing, we're always going to choose to focus. Why not do this on purpose?

In the past, you had unintentional *distraction blackouts*—a forced period of time where you have no choice but to ignore all your usual distractions. It's obvious that this will lead to high productivity and focus, so let's make it a habit to regularly schedule distraction blackouts.

All you need to do is block out an entire afternoon—at least two, but no more than four hours—and deprive yourself of any other distractions so you are literally forced to work on a task. Turn your phone on silent (actually, turn it off and leave it at home), turn your Wi-Fi off, don't rearrange your desk or office, and don't you dare procrastinate otherwise. Sit in an empty room with a single desk and chair if you have to. Some people wear earplugs.

Gather only what you need to occupy yourself for the next two to four hours, and nothing else that you would find interesting whatsoever. The point of the distraction blackout is to force you into a zone where you have no choice but to work. I know it's hard; you are forcing yourself into an uncomfortable situation for the greater good.

You are put in a position where you have two choices: to sit staring blankly and stupidly, wasting time, or to begrudgingly do something productive. It's the ultimate *I might as well* situation.

Once you're in the blackout, you can ramp up your productivity by competing against yourself.

Make it a game of accomplishment by measuring your output at the top of every hour. Competition is one of the most motivating factors, no matter who you are competing with, because your pride is on the line.

You are racing against the clock and yourself. Work is not inherently motivating, so let's say you plan to edit 20,000 words during a blackout. If you only edited 5,000 words the first hour, you'd better do at least 6,500 the next hour. Whatever you accomplished in the first hour (or day, or distraction blackout), try to top yourself in the next period. This will prove surprisingly addicting and ramp up your efficiency.

Make sure your list of objectives for that blackout is longer than you think you might be able to complete. If your blackout is going to be three hours, include what you think would amount to five hours of work. The reality is that what could be five hours of work *outside* a blackout may really only be three hours of distraction-free work. You'll be surprised what you can accomplish when you are in the zone. Create this game plan before the fact so you can reach for the next task as you finish your current one.

Finally, you should schedule your distraction blackouts for your most productive timeframe of the day.

You might notice that some parts of your day are always more productive than others. Some of us are night owls while others are morning birds. Most people naturally have peak performance hours when they are more alert and sharp, no matter what the context. As a result, the work we produce is better and needs less editing during those periods.

For example, my optimal time to schedule a distraction blackout is late afternoon or after dinner. I simply function better later in the day, and perhaps don't fully wake up until then. It doesn't matter what I've done during the day before that period of time; I can produce more at fifty percent mental capacity during those time periods than one hundred percent mental capacity earlier in the day, most of the time.

Figuring out your peak productivity hours and combining them with distraction blackouts is a productivity double whammy. You'll be exponentially focused and alert if you pair them together, and knock out tasks on your lists at a rate you've never worked at before.

Regardless of how long your peak productivity times are and where they occur, during your day, you need to take advantage of them. You don't want to waste this highly productive "sweet spot" playing video games or answering emails. Talk about wasted resources! Instead, plan for maximum productivity during these times.

There is an extra benefit to a distraction blackout, and that is the level of deep thought you are able to devote to a single subject or topic. You're able to think about it beyond the primary concerns you normally only see in passing, and can think at the secondary and tertiary levels. You'll be able to visualize all the connections between topics and tasks in a new light, and your creativity will be awakened. I frequently come up with spontaneous ideas for improvements, new projects, and exploring things I'm thinking about, or working on more deeply during a distraction blackout.

You aren't able to truly delve into a topic if you are constantly distracted. You'll understand the surface level, but only sitting, fixating, and focusing for extended periods of time will provide the sorts of insights and realizations that will move the needle for you.

Takeaways:

- Momentum is a delicate thing. While the first section was focused on getting started, this section is on step two, three, and four, and making sure you capitalize on your hot start. Momentum by itself may be easier to achieve than breaking inertia, but it can slip away in just a moment.
- An easy way for momentum to slip away is through perfectionist tendencies. Perfectionism is nitpicking at every small detail at the detriment of overall progress. It emphasizes quality over quantity—this by itself isn't negative, but all things in moderation. To boot, the main reason most people engage in perfectionism isn't because of an adherence to excellence—it is because of fear of judgment and rejection.
- Perfectionism will halt you in your steps. So will constantly doubling back and editing, correcting, and tweaking things before you

finish one hundred percent of something. Do and complete first, edit later. This doesn't just apply to writing. When you go back to fix or change something, you lose your train of thought and cease to keep going forward. You begin to slide backward, and by the time you finish editing, you've taken one step forward and two steps back. Completion is almost always your real goal.

- Multitasking is a myth. We've all heard this, but it's time to hear it again. We know that trying to work on several things simultaneously just results in poor quality across the board—most of us avoid this, at this point. However, we still tend to switch between tasks frequently, which is the modern version of multitasking. It takes far longer than you might expect to shrug off a distraction and return to your previous mental state, so defeat multitasking by single-tasking and focusing. If you feel that you need to address something during your single-tasking period, just write it on a distractions list and don't confuse something that's urgent for something that's important.

- Get in the habit of taking notes in general— this simple act frees up your brain for the present moment and doesn't let the future or the past interfere.

- Finally, distraction blackouts can increase your momentum because they force you into a state of boredom and isolation. When you're bored, you have a choice to remain bored, or begrudgingly work on what's in front of you. Intentionally put yourself into an uncomfortable situation, and you'll come out the other side in a better position. Use competition against yourself as an additional motivator. Make sure to schedule a distraction blackout during your time of greatest daily energy and efficiency.

Chapter 7: Making Time Your Friend

"Time management is a misnomer. The challenge is to manage ourselves."

- Stephen R. Covey

Time. Is it your best friend, or your worst enemy?

When you're doing something you love, it's your worst enemy because it always seems to run out too soon, and you never seem to have enough. When you're doing something you hate, it's your best friend because it's the only thing keeping you from freedom and pleasure. Or is it the other way around?

No matter the case, time is what you're going to have to deal with if you want to improve your focus and productivity. Whether you believe you have too much of it, too little, or just the right amount, you'll need to start thinking about it in ways you never have before.

Time will always keep on running, but how can we change our perspective to be more focused, productive, and determined?

Protect Your Time

Being productive, effective, and successful in life means having a healthy relationship to time, which, when you think about it, is your most precious resource. Without it, nothing gets done, and when your time on this earth eventually runs out, no excuse or justification or bargain will buy you any more of it. Being productive means *making the most of your time*—but as for how much time you have, well, that's fixed.

Now consider that many people are accidentally and unconsciously selfish. They'll ask things of you and not offer to reciprocate, often thinking nothing of it. Of course, most people are relatively subtle about this, or we would disown most of our friends. You might even do it yourself.

The biggest way people subtly, and sometimes unknowingly, act selfishly is when they monopolize your time. When given the opportunity, many of your friends or coworkers will hog your time and leave little for your own tasks and interests. Your time is a precious and finite resource, and yet they'll treat it as though it's worthless and infinite.

It could be as simple as guilt-tripping you to come to an event, trapping you in conversations that are entirely about them, or inviting you for coffee to "*pick your brain.*" These are all selfish motivations that you've likely wanted to avoid and find a way out of before.

To punch out procrastination and extend your focus, you need to take your time back from other people. You'll need to start protecting it as a means to protecting your focus. Note here that it's not about them, it's about *you* and what you do to protect your own time.

It's tough to say no to your friends, but if you spend all of your time doing things you feel obligated to do, people simply won't respect your time. They may still respect you, but they'll know they can have you there at a moment's notice, and they will take you for granted.

Luckily, you can do this in a very diplomatic way. To make people respect your time and earn more freedom for yourself, *make others act first.*

Instead of flat-out refusing their request for your time, or telling them to leave your vicinity (two awkward options at best), create a *small hoop* that people have to jump through before you actually give them your time. You are acting as your own gatekeeper in a sense.

The best way I've managed to put this into practice is with a pre-meeting email or act. If someone wants an uninterrupted block of my time and I think it might be detrimental to my focus or productivity, I ask them to follow up with me via email about their concern or question *before* I actually meet with them, and I'll get back to them when I can.

This accomplishes two things: It allows me to continue uninterrupted, and it puts the burden of action on someone else and allows me to sit back and wait. This also applies when people ask me to attend events I'm not so keen on, so you can use it in both your personal and professional life.

I've found this simple condition weeds out the majority of requests for my time simply because most people can't be bothered to send me the requested email about their question. Well, if they can't be bothered to spend five minutes doing something for me, why would I spend an hour with them?

If they aren't willing to do that, then it clearly wasn't a burning question that would have led to a productive conversation. It would have been entirely for their benefit or just a complete waste of my time.

Since this actually weeds out the majority of people who want to utilize my time, it's my diplomatic way of saying no. Even with most of the people who do actually send the pre-meeting email, I can answer their questions with a few written sentences and it saves both of our time . . . especially mine because it forced them to accurately define their questions.

Out of ten potential coffee meetings, three might actually follow up via email, and I'll be able to quickly and efficiently answer two out of those three questions via email. This turns ten meetings into one, which is a great win for your productivity and getting people to respect your time. I've also pinpointed the people I can really help in an in-depth way.

Now, it's not that I mind meeting with people who want help. I've had a lot of help along the way, and many of those same coffee meetings have been invaluable to my personal and professional growth. I love helping people whenever I can, but I simply can't afford to indulge everyone who wants to chat at the expense of my own daily output. And neither can you: you have your daily priorities, so don't become a part of someone else's to-do list.

This is a book about maximizing your focus, and these are the steps you must implement in your life to make the most of your every waking hour!

Applying a specific process to gaining actual face-time with you will make people aware that you are indeed busy. There are certainly times for meeting new people, but it's not when you're trying to maximize your productivity.

All you're doing is making people aware of the schedule you're working in. They can work their way into it, and if they want to just hang out and indulge themselves, they have to do so outside of that schedule.

If people want something from you, they should be willing to work for it. It's more than common courtesy; it's common sense. If you do someone a favor, they should put in as much of the legwork as possible and make it easy for you to complete.

What about when people just show up in your office, at your door, in your cubicle, or at your lunch table unannounced? How can you protect your time then?

That's when we need to talk about how direct you want to be. If you don't mind being direct, then you don't really need to seek advice here. You already know what to do. But if you're like ninety-nine percent of the population, the very idea of being so direct in a negative manner makes you anxious.

Let's say that you're working hard at your desk and your resident chatterbox sits down next to you. What's your first move?

"Hey, nice to see you. Just to let you know I'm working on this and need to concentrate soon, so I can only spare a couple of minutes right now . . . until about 10:40." In this scenario, it's 10:36.

For the serial violator, this simple statement at the outset is to set the tone and set up your escape route at the beginning instead of the end—because we all know it can be tough to squeeze those words out at the end of a conversation. If you just preempt the problem, you give yourself a clear exit.

If your violator doesn't instantly leave and catch you later, then you have free rein to look at your watch or phone and mention the time in a surprised and shocked manner. For instance, "Oh, wow, it's already 10:42! Okay, I need to get back to this. Can I catch up with you later?"

Make a show of looking at the time and emphasizing its importance. This should in theory cue your violator to leave. Make sure to add the touch of asking people for permission to find them later—no one will ever say no to that request, and it lets you come off as generous. You can even add an addendum of not wanting to be rude and apologizing for being so busy and such.

People don't understand subtle hints—or at least, the people that you want to leave never will—so protecting your time is a matter of saying exactly what you mean without an impolite impact. It's easy to miss the mark because you're essentially saying, "I don't want to see you right now," but that's not personal and doesn't mean you *never* want to see them. It's about conveying that you've just reached your limits and need to prioritize yourself for the time being.

Protect your time, because time is opportunity, money, pleasure, and everything good in your life. In fact, what's the most valuable possession you own? It's not anything material—it's your time.

Time is the one asset that you will never be able to get back, make up for, or replace. Once the minute you spend reading this sentence passes, you'll never get it back (but of course, reading this sentence is a minute well-spent).

Time gives you *opportunity*.

Each new minute you're alive, you have the opportunity to do something. You can choose from an infinite number of choices. You can plan ahead, work on something, communicate with people, entertain yourself, or eat. There are so many possibilities when you have time at your disposal.

Once that block of time is gone, it's gone forever. You can't hop on a time machine and get it back. It is finite. You only get one bite of the apple. The sun won't always rise the next day, and you don't want to be asking yourself what you could have done differently each day.

Protect your time and cherish it. Make sure you're doing exactly what you want, within reason. A significant part of this is not squandering your time with choices that appear to be necessary, but actually suck up your happiness and opportunities.

Don't do things out of obligation. When you feel obligated to do something, that means you don't see your own happiness or benefit in it. It is solely for someone else's benefit, and it provides little or no value for you. You're probably just acting to avoid guilt or other negative feelings.

Some might say it is selfless and giving, but remember your own time is worth more than gold! If you're putting other people at a higher priority than you are yourself, it will just lead to unhappiness and a sense of waste.

If you feel there are other more important and pressing things you should be doing, do those instead. If you simply don't want to do something, don't do it. If you know you're not going to be happy doing something or going somewhere, evaluate where your priorities should lie.

Don't spend time with negative people. Negative people suck out your energy. They are motivation vampires. In many cases, misery loves company. They are negative, and they just want other people to be negative as well. They look at life as a horrible ordeal they need to get through, and nothing makes them happier than turning otherwise positive people into people like them.

It's damaging to your productivity and to your quality of life.

Likewise, if you don't feel excited to see someone, it's a strong sign you could be using your time in a way that makes you happier, and thus more productive. Much of the time, we never realize that someone is a drag on us until we take a step back and really think. They may be important people in our lives, but if they make you annoyed, frustrated, or unhappy after seeing them, then what is the point of the relationship?

Maximize your leisure time. Taking advantage of your time isn't all about maximizing your productivity or avoiding activities that don't add value to your life.

It's also about maximizing your leisure time, and making sure you enjoy the free time you do have in the way you want to enjoy it. This means that instead of squandering an afternoon watching golf and snoozing on your couch, you should take note of your favorite activities and hobbies and proactively schedule them for your free time!

Valuing your time is the ultimate precursor to productivity.

Parkinson Knows

Do you remember Parkinson from a previous chapter? Parkinson's Law states that *work expands so as to fill the time available for its completion.* Well, Cyril Parkinson was a man of many talents, but for the purposes of this section, we'll focus on a second of his laws that was eventually named after him, called *Parkinson's Law of Triviality,* also known as the bike shed effect.

The story behind the law is that there was a committee tasked with designing a nuclear power plant. This was obviously a large undertaking, so appropriate care had to be taken in addressing the safety mechanisms and environmental implications of building a new nuclear power plant.

The committee met regularly and was able to quell most safety and environmental concerns. They were even able to ensure the nuclear power plant had a pleasing aesthetic that would surely attract the best engineers.

However, as the committee met to deal with the remaining issues, one issue in particular kept popping up: the design of the bike shed for employees that commuted by bicycle.

This included the color, the signage, the materials used, and the type of bike rack to be installed. The committee couldn't get past these details—details that were meaningless in the greater scope of a functioning nuclear power plant. They kept fixating on small, trivial features that were a matter of opinion and subjectivity.

Therein lies the essence of Parkinson's Law of Triviality. People are prone to overthinking and fixating on small details that don't matter in the grand scheme of a task, and they do so to the detriment of larger issues that have infinitely more importance. These are the tasks that, if you were to take a step back and evaluate, would compel you to ask, "*Who the heck cares about this?*"

When you lack the clarity and focus to really tackle your big objectives, you start addressing tasks to fit your level of mental energy. You let your tasks run you. It's the classic case of not being able to see the forest for the trees and unwittingly keeping yourself from the finish line. This is especially pronounced when a group is collectively making a decision. Why?

There are two main reasons for this phenomenon.

The first reason is procrastination and avoidance. When people want to procrastinate on an issue, they often try to remain productive by doing something that is perceived as productive. Trivial details are still details that need to be taken care of at some point, and they are things that we can tweak endlessly.

This is why we clean when we are putting off work. We're subconsciously avoiding the work, but making ourselves feel better by thinking, "*At least something productive got done!*"

Fixating on the trivial is the equivalent of cleaning the bathroom to avoid work. You are being productive in some way, but not in a way that aids your overall goal. That's why when the committee members were stuck on how to tackle all of the safety issues, they defaulted to something they *could* theoretically solve: a bike shed.

Trivial tasks need to be addressed at some point, but you need to evaluate when you should actually address them. Triviality can easily sneak into our lives as a placebo for real productivity.

Second, and this refers more to group situations, the Law of Triviality may be the result of individuals who wish to contribute in any way they can but find themselves unable to in all but the most trivial of matters. They're on the committee, but they don't have the knowledge or expertise to contribute to more significant issues.

Yet everyone can visualize a cheap, simple bicycle shed, so planning one can result in endless discussions, because everyone involved wants to add a touch and show personal contribution. It's completely self-serving.

The main and only reason to call meetings is to solve big problems that require input from multiple people. Locking people in a room and letting them brainstorm is a fairly proven method for getting things done—*if* you have an agenda that you stick to. Anything else should be addressed independently; otherwise, the level of discussion inevitably falls to the lowest common denominator in the room.

If somebody starts talking about something that's not on the agenda, you know that triviality is on your doorstep. If somebody is spinning their wheels regarding a tiny aspect of a larger project, triviality is already in the room. If you find yourself suddenly compelled to organize your sock drawer while working on a particularly tough issue, triviality has made a cup of tea and is making itself comfortable.

Be on the lookout for these patterns. When you devolve into small tasks that may not need tweaking, or do not impact your overall goal, it's time to take a break and recharge instead of pretending to be productive.

The key to combatting triviality is threefold: (1) have a strict agenda, whether it is your to-do list or calendar or other technique, so you know what you should focus on and what you should ignore; (2) know your overall goals for the day and constantly ask yourself if what you're doing is contributing to them or avoiding them; and (3) develop an awareness of when you're starting to lose energy so you can pre-empt triviality from occurring.

Knowing is half the battle when it comes to beating Parkinson's Law of Triviality.

Parkinson's other law, as we've already seen, is simply known as *Parkinson's Law* and is arguably more well-known. One of the things that people who procrastinate a lot might say to justify it is that they work better under a time crunch—"I work best with a deadline!"

Parkinson's Law states that *work expands so as to fill the time available for its completion*. Whatever deadline you give yourself, big or small, that's how long you'll take to complete work. If you give yourself a relaxed deadline, you avoid being disciplined; if you give yourself a tight deadline, you can draw on your self-discipline.

Parkinson observed that as bureaucracies expanded, their efficiency decreased instead of increased. The more space and time people were given, the more they took—something that he realized was applicable to a wide range of other circumstances. The general form of the law became that increasing the size of something decreases its efficiency.

As it relates to focus and time, Parkinson found that simple tasks would be made increasingly more complex in order to fill the time allotted to their completion. Decreasing the available time for completing a task caused that task to become simpler and easier and completed in a more timely fashion.

Building on Parkinson's Law, a study of college students found that those who imposed strict deadlines on themselves for completing assignments consistently performed better than those who gave themselves an excessive amount of time and those who set no limits at all. Why? The artificial limitations they had set for their work caused them to be far more efficient than their counterparts. They didn't spend a lot of time worrying about the assignments because they didn't give themselves the time to indulge. They got to work, finished the projects, and moved on. They also didn't have time to ruminate on what ultimately didn't matter—a very common type of subtle procrastination. They were able to subconsciously focus on only the elements that mattered in completing the assignment.

Very few people are ever going to require you or even ask you to work less. So if you want to be more productive and efficient, you'll have to avoid falling victim to Parkinson's Law yourself by applying artificial limitations on the time you give yourself to complete tasks. By simply giving yourself time limits and deadlines for your work, you force yourself to focus on the crucial elements of the task. You don't make things more complex or difficult than they need to be just to fill the time.

For example, say that your supervisor gives you a spreadsheet and asks you to make a few charts from it by the end of the week. The task might take an hour, but after looking over the spreadsheet you notice that it's disorganized and difficult to read, so you start editing it. This takes an entire week, but the charts you were supposed to generate would only have taken an hour. If you had been given the deadline of one day, you would have simply focused on the charts and ignored everything that wasn't important. When we are given the space, as Parkinson's Law dictates, we expand our work to fill the time.

Set aggressive deadlines so that you are actually challenging yourself on a consistent basis, and you'll avoid this pitfall. A distant deadline also typically means a sustained level of background stress—push yourself to finish early and free your mind. Save your time by giving yourself less time. Sounds easy, doesn't it?

In many ways, the principles of prioritizing action, seizing momentum, and trimming down options to kill decision fatigue are all ways of deliberately setting up limitations that will focus the mind and get you moving forward, just like Parkinson's two laws. It's all about remembering that time is not infinite—if we hope to achieve something, we need to budget our time and use it wisely.

The Pareto Principle

Let's look at another strategy that will help you place time management at the core of your approach. Back when I was starting my own business, I spent a lot of time spinning my wheels on tasks that didn't matter. This can easily spiral into perfectionism and analysis paralysis, and I was no exception.

Because I wanted everything I produced to impart as much value as possible, I spent an inordinate amount of time on small changes and edits that no one besides me would ever notice. I suppose my head was in the right place, but that's not what makes a business succeed.

The overall message and effectiveness were largely the same, but I would re-work sentences over and over until I was satisfied with them. Consequently, it took almost a year to write and edit my first book.

This isn't to say that quality control isn't important. However, I now realize there's no sense in agonizing over every word choice in a book, especially if the overall message and effectiveness will not change or be improved. As we saw in our section on perfectionism, we can succumb to the illusion that endless refining and tweaking is improving things, when all it's doing is delaying valuable action and wasting time.

In the vast majority of cases, tinkering with the tiny things won't make a difference. The primary reason is the 80/20 Rule, otherwise known as the Pareto Principle.

The Pareto Principle was named for an Italian economist who accurately noted that eighty percent of the real estate in Italy was owned by only twenty percent of the population. He began to wonder if the same kind of distribution applied to other aspects of life. In fact, he was correct.

The Pareto Principle applies to everything about the human experience: our work, relationships, career, grades, hobbies, and interests. Time is your most precious asset, and the Pareto Principle allows you to use it more effectively for maximum rewards. It accurately recognizes that you just might be wasting a significant amount of time on things that make no difference.

The Pareto Principle states that eighty percent of the results you want out of a task will be produced by twenty percent of your activities and efforts directed toward it.

In other words, only twenty percent of the tasks you perform toward a certain goal will account for the vast majority of your results. Conversely, the remaining eight percent of the tasks and effort are merely focused on bringing a task to perfection and optimal efficiency. They are mostly unnecessary in the name of high productivity and output, and most of the time they are not worth the effort. Talk about a waste.

In concrete terms, twenty percent of the tasks you focus on will yield eighty percent of the results you desire, and any additional tasks you might focus on aren't going to impact your overall productivity that much. Further, twenty percent of the time you spend on a task will yield eighty percent of the progress you need, and any additional time spent will create diminishing returns and an overall poor usage of your time.

The tip has a simple proposition: pay attention to only twenty percent of your tasks, and for those tasks, twenty percent of the effort you spend on them just might be sufficient for your purposes.

For example, if you set a goal of trying to lose weight, you will lose eighty percent of the weight by just doing twenty percent of the actions you think you should, such as eating within certain hours and hitting the gym three times a week. Everything else, like counting every calorie and lugging around Tupperware filled with broccoli and chicken—that's the eighty percent effort that will only create twenty percent of the results. Further, twenty percent of the time spent on losing weight will yield the bulk of the results, and any more time spent is unnecessary unless you are trying to drop to four percent body fat.

You would just focus on the actions that make the biggest impact and debate whether you want to even touch the others. Seek the biggest bang for your buck. What are the tasks that make the biggest impact, regardless of details or completion? Do those first and foremost—they might be all you need.

Lacking awareness of this phenomenon means you will continue to spin your wheels on eighty percent of the effort that doesn't impact your bottom line. You will also fail to identify the twenty percent of your business, tasks, or work that are truly working for you and miss a host of opportunities. This is when time works *against* you.

To maximize your focus, you need to realize there is a point at which working on something won't yield any more results. There's a point beyond which people won't notice the additional work or perfection, and where the purpose of the task is adequately satisfied. For most of us, this point is far earlier and lower than we might expect.

Here's an illustration of how the Pareto Principle impacts real life application.

Language expert Gabriel Wyner says that when you're beginning to learn a new language, focus only on the thousand or so most common words in that language first: "After one thousand words, you'll know seventy percent of the words in any average text, and two thousand words provide you with eighty percent text coverage."

Wyner explains the imbalance even further. Let's say you knew only ten English words: "the," "(to) be," "of," "and," "a," "to," "in," "he," "have," and "it." If that was the extent of your vocabulary, how much of any text would you recognize?

According to Dr. Paul Nation, the answer is 23.7%. Those ten words represent 0.00004% of the English language, which has over 250,000 words. But we use those ten so often that they regularly make up nearly twenty-five percent of every sentence we write.

Let's say we eventually increase our vocabulary to a whopping one hundred words—including "year," "(to) see," "(to) give," "then," "most," "great," "(to) think," and "there." With that number, Dr. Nation says, we'd have the ability to understand forty-nine percent of every sentence uttered.

Let that sink in a bit—with only one hundred words, we can recognize nearly half the content of every sentence. Let's be generous and fluff his numbers—that would still mean that with two hundred words, we could recognize forty percent of the content in each sentence. The fact that *less than one ten-thousandth* of all English words make of almost half of every sentence is kind of a big deal. That is a staggering demonstration of the Pareto Principle.

What tasks do you *really* think people will or won't notice (even if you do)? What additional tasks might others tell you to just skip or disregard? How can you maximize your efficiency by knowing where to cut corners? How can you manage your energy and save your focus for what really matters?

Focus and productivity are never about your best intentions. They are purely results-driven, and the Pareto Principle drives results in the most efficient manner with the time you have.

Maker and Manager Modes

What's a maker and what's a manager? Well, chances are you constantly juggle both roles despite your actual title.

When you're writing a report or analyzing a document, you're a maker. It's when you are producing and creating something—anything. On the other hand, when you're coordinating, planning, or scheduling, you're acting like a manager. You may not have realized it, but these are diametrically opposed roles. To start with, one requires uninterrupted time, while the other one is specifically trying to interrupt schedules.

Consider the daily schedule of novelist Haruki Murakami. When he's working on a novel, he starts his days at 4:00 a.m. and writes for five or six continuous hours. This is his maker mode. Once the writing is done, he spends his afternoons exercising and coordinating with others, and his evenings reading or listening to music before his 9:00 p.m. bedtime. Of course, he spends the rest of his day in manager mode. Why is this so significant?

Paul Graham of technology incubator Y Combinator first described this concept in a 2009 essay. From Graham's distinction between makers and managers, we can learn that doing creative work or overseeing other people does not necessitate certain habits or routines. It requires consideration of the way we structure our time. Namely, it requires us to recognize when we are in either mode and then split our days accordingly like Murakami.

A manager's day is, as a rule, sliced up into tiny slots, each with a specific purpose decided in advance. Managers spend a lot of time "putting out fires" and doing reactive work. An important call or email comes in, so it gets answered. To focus on one task for a substantial block of time, managers need to make an effort to prevent other people from distracting them.

A maker's schedule is the polar opposite. It is made up of long blocks of time reserved for focusing on particular tasks, or the entire day might be devoted to one activity. Breaking their day up into slots consisting of a few minutes each would be the equivalent of doing nothing. They need to do one thing well and can leave the rest to the managers. Uninterrupted time is truly the currency for a maker.

When you try to mix and match these two modes throughout your day, both modes won't be able to accomplish what they want. Not even close.

For improved focus, alter your schedule to ensure that you are keeping everything maker related together and everything manager related together. In other words, you should batch the tasks from each mode together so each mode can actually accomplish what they want.

If you have three documents to write and three meetings (interruptions) to hold, how might you structure your day? Suppose you held meetings one hour apart—does that give the maker enough time to get into the zone and create? No. Or, suppose you keep the meetings one right after the other—does that give the manager enough time to react and organize? No.

A better method would be to emulate what Murakami does by devoting your mornings to writing and then your afternoons to meetings.

We all embody these roles from time to time, so set each version of yourself up for success by differentiating and batching maker and manager modes. However you end up managing your daily schedule and the roles you take on, what's important is that you're able to zoom out and see the bigger picture, as well as how everything fits in time-wise.

Just Ten Minutes

Let's recap a little. We know that we only have finite time to achieve our goals and do what we need to do. We also know that our own brains are often wired up to work against these goals. It would seem that the challenge is to make the best of our cognitive abilities and work around our blind spots and weaknesses, all within the time we have available.

In each precious moment, how can we tap into our inner reserves of focus? Our tendency to procrastinate on large or intimidating projects has biological roots but is reinforced, as we've seen, by our own attitudes, mindsets, and beliefs. We visualize the worst parts of the task, adding layers of emotion each time we picture ourselves performing it, and that makes it easier to delay getting started. But we can overcome this inertia and reclaim that precious time by implementing the ten-minute rule.

The rule is simple: just commit to starting and sticking with it for ten minutes. Remember, the key is just to start. Time is magnificent, endless, and a puzzle—but we can take it ten minutes at a time and drastically improve our focus.

That's where the ten-minute rule comes in. There are two main ways to use it:

If you want something, wait at least ten minutes before getting it. It's simple and leaves no room for debate or excuses. When you feel an urge, force yourself to wait for ten minutes before giving in to whatever the urge is. If you're still craving it after ten minutes, then have it, or wait ten more minutes because you've already done it and survived just fine. Simply by choosing to wait, you remove the "immediate" from immediate gratification, thereby building focus and discipline.

Similarly, if you want to quit something beneficial, wait just ten more minutes. It's the same thought process applied in a different way. Ten minutes is nothing, so you can wait or continue that long easily. Then, if you do it once, it's easy to repeat, isn't it?

For example, if you'd rather not do the dishes or your homework, that's exactly what you're going to do for at least ten minutes. You can give yourself permission to quit after ten measly minutes. Chances are you'll finish the task you were dreading, or eliminate the inertia that was holding you back and not want to stop after ten minutes. Perfect.

The secret sauce is in immediate action. If you're able to cross this threshold, you'll see that the task itself is not so painful. It was just your sense of laziness and sloth that was holding you back.

You'll surprise yourself with how much more you can get done and how easy it is to build your sense of willpower. The difficult part is creating the snowball, but we all know what happens when you roll it down a hill.

Takeaways:

- The concept of time is intertwined with focus and productivity. Mostly, we see this relationship as negative because we always seem to be lacking time. But there are a few ways to reset your perspective of time and understand how it can help you, rather than hurt you.
- Protect your time. Your time is precious, and only when you can protect it from others will you realize its true value. You can ward people off who threaten your focus by making them jump through a small hoop to speak in depth with you. If you are

ambushed in person, set the tone at preemptively mention that you are busy and have very little time to spare.

- Make the most out of your time by not doing things out of obligation or duty, avoiding negative people no matter their relationship to you, and maximizing your limited leisure time by not being lazy and doing what makes you happiest.

- Parkinson came up with two important laws related to focus and time. First is Parkinson's Law of Triviality, which states that you must see the forest through the trees and not get stuck in small details because they are easy to brainstorm with and kick around. Parkinson's second law is known simply as Parkinson's Law and states that work expands to fill the time it is given. To battle this, proactively set aggressive deadlines and don't allow yourself to be seduced by seemingly free time.

- Manage your maker and manager modes. When you're a maker, you're creating something. When you're a manger, you're coordinating, planning, scheduling, and informing. These are polar opposites in terms of what they require, and thus, you should be aware of the mode you're currently in and batch your mode-specific tasks together.

- Just ten minutes; that's all it takes sometimes to build focus and jumpstart productivity. If you don't feel like getting started, commit to just ten minutes. If you feel like quitting, persevere for just ten minutes. That's all it takes.

Chapter 8: Tips for Making Productivity a Lifelong Habit

"We are what we repeatedly do. Success is not an action but a habit."

- Aristotle

Keep a Distraction List to Stay Focused

With emails, social media, and a thousand little to-dos, it's easy to get distracted when you're trying to be productive. In fact, so much of our world today is *designed* to be distracting—advertisements constantly vie for your attention and threaten to make you forget all the grand plans and promises you had only a moment earlier.

Whether you're trying to focus on deep work or just dealing with smaller tasks, distractions are the bane of productivity. And here's the thing: they're not going away. It's hard to maintain efficient work habits with distractions around, but on the other hand there will always be *something* to distract you; it's just life.

One powerful method of reducing distractions is creating a "distraction list." This is a tool that will help you be as effective as possible in a world bursting with distractions. It's simple: whenever a distracting thought pops up, write it down on the list and get back to work. Keep your list (whether it's a Google Doc or a physical piece of paper) nearby while you're working. It's not that you're valiantly trying to ignore them or force them out of your mind, but rather that you acknowledge them and essentially set them aside until later.

Let's define what a "distraction" really is—any intrusive and seemingly uncontrolled thought that "pops up" in your mind and temporarily takes you away from the moment you were focusing on. Yes, this could be an annoying notification on your phone or the doorbell, but more often distractions come purely form within our own minds:

"Remember that your parents are visiting on Friday and you need to buy some wine."

"Don't forget to call the GP about your mole."

"You've got a deadline tomorrow."

"When are you going to find time to do that workout?"

A distraction can come from the external environment, but they are usually more numerous and more damaging when they come in the form of a steady stream of thoughts that interfere with your attention and workflow. The technique is simple: have a pen and paper at hand beside you when you're working, and the very second one of these thoughts pops up, quickly scribble it down as it appears in your mind.

Tell yourself that once it's written down on your distraction list, your brain no longer needs to constantly remind you of it. You can carry on working. When you're done your work session, review your list. Chances are there will be some things on there that are just pointless worries and ruminations. Cross these off. Look at other thoughts and decide what **action** you can take to remove it from the list. Worrying is useless; action moves things along.

If you've written down "You've got a deadline tomorrow," then make a plan to address that. Are you on target to reach the deadline? What do you need to do to get there? Could you set a reminder, schedule extra work, delegate, or ask for an extension?

The distraction list seems simple, but it works. Thoughts that anxiously "pop up" are often

219

your brain's way of helping you remember things. In fact, so much of our worry can be eliminated if we take the time to note these reminders, and again, take *action* on them so our minds can rest. It's normal for these inbuilt reminders to pop up at all times, but a simple writing down technique can help us shape and control this impulse into something that actually makes us more effective and focused.

A distraction list is a little like an offsite memory that reduces your cognitive load. You are reassuring your brain that you have remembered, and that it can stop sending you random alerts throughout your workday! As you write something down, mentally tell yourself that you will address it later at a pre-defined time. This calms you down and builds a sense of trust in your own organizational competence—you're not forgetting anything, and all your tasks will be tended to at the right time.

You can play around with this technique, but make sure you're including two key steps:

Step 1: immediately write down a distraction as it pops up in your head

Step 2: review the list at your own pace later and take ACTION where you can.

Make Fewer Decisions (About Things that aren't Important)

Some decisions are important. Most aren't. Every day, we are bombarded with options and possibilities and getting bogged down in them is now commonly recognized as "decision fatigue." Your mental bandwidth, willpower, and attention are not infinite resources—they get depleted with use. It makes sense, then, that if you want to be more productive, consider outsourcing or eliminating everyday choices. Consider all your choices and decisions in terms of their priority—truly big and important decisions are something to deliberate on. But ordinary, everyday things that don't make much difference? They're not important and can be ignored, delegated, or automated to free up your brainpower.

Sometimes, you procrastinate on making a decision that, if you're honest with yourself, *doesn't matter at all.* You're overloaded and finding it hard to be productive, but then, so much of the load you're carrying is insignificant in the grand scheme of things. Decision fatigue is often a powerful driver of procrastination. There are an estimated thirty-five thousand decisions we each make every—and each one could be directly sapping your productivity.

There are three ways to trim down frivolous decisions that eat up time and energy:

1. Have a solid understanding of what's important and what isn't (hint: most of it isn't)
2. Use that understanding to prioritize and focus your energy on where it matters most
3. Simply reduce the number of decisions you make, period

Habit and routine can help, as can having a fixed procedure for decision-making that reflects your values—because these approaches take decisions out of your hands and free up your brainpower. So, what does that look like in practical terms? It's all about making the right thing easy and automatic.

For example, have a morning wake-up alarm that never changes, not even on the weekends. If you're completely in the habit of waking up at the same time day after day, you don't spend any extra effort forcing yourself out of bed in the mornings. It just happens. One more decision you don't have to make. Instead of wasting time everyday deciding on an outfit to wear, design a kind of "uniform" for yourself where you cycle through a limited number of outfits you already know work for you, or close variations. This helps you wake up and get dressed without too much deliberation.

By the same token, don't answer the question "what's for dinner?" over and over again—you could have two weeks' worth of favorite recipes you cycle through so you don't have to waste time planning, shopping, or cooking anything new. Another trick is to batch cook so that you essentially make two or more decisions when you simply make one. What's for dinner? You already decided in the past, so there's nothing to think about and plan. Again, you get more done with fewer decisions.

Organization is a way to tidy and streamline your *mental* space, not just your physical space. If you plan ahead, you are sparing your future self the mental effort of having to reinvent the wheel over and over. Schedule your exercise at the same time everyday so it becomes habitual. Take a few minutes in the evening to plan your work schedule for the following day. Stick to the same brands, colors of clothing, meals, or routes. Make a list of staples you always use, or compile a media list so you're not wasting time wondering what to read or watch next. Put as much as possible on autopilot. *The more you can replace each individual decision with a process or a habit, the better.*

Another way to make sure you're making fewer decisions is to get really clear and honest about your priorities. Do you *really* need to do XYZ?

Why? Something may certainly be important, but then, is it absolutely necessary that *you* do it? You could always delegate. If you're working with others, practice trusting them to do what they're there to do, rather than assuming that everything will fall apart unless you micromanage every little detail for them. Look at your life and see where anything looks complicated or takes a lot of processing power to work through, then see what you can do to streamline everything and make it run without your mental input. Fewer decisions = simplicity = focus.

Create a System

As we've seen, habits and processes are more efficient since they get things done automatically and without drawing too much cognitive effort from us. However, you've probably developed a few productivity-ruining habits over the years—this is a huge opportunity loss, since those same habits could be working for you instead of against you.

Manage distraction and procrastination by creating a system. When you bumble through your day without a plan or a strategy, you are basically expecting the right thing to happen by accident. But with a system you take conscious control, you pre-empt, and you automate in ways that really count.

But first, let's get honest: how many times have you read about a productivity tool or installed a productivity app only to discover it did precisely zero for your life or even worse, actually got in the way? These tools can help us make decisions, communicate, plan, solve problems, and stay organized—but we still need to have a solid plan for how to integrate them into your lives. Productivity tools are not magic bullets that you simply tack onto your life. They need to *fit*. A poorly used productivity tool is worse than useless, and it's certainly worse than no tool at all. You need a complete system that realistically incorporates the right tool into your life.

Sounds good, but what does that really look like?

To build a productivity system from the ground up, you need to focus on two key features:

WHY and

WHEN

The right system is one that works for you and the goals you want to achieve. It takes into account your unique limits and constraints. If a system isn't actually making your life easier? Then it's not a good system. Drop it. Yes, even if Steve Jobs or whoever supposedly used it!

Making a good system takes time and effort, but don't think it's super complicated. Try the following:

Step 1: Make time.

It won't happen by accident. You need to set aside a time to get organized. As an example, many people dedicate a few hours on Sunday evening to review and plan the week ahead.

Step 2: Make a plan

First review the week past (or, if you like, go for shorter chunks, e.g., daily). Look at what worked and what didn't. Ask WHY something worked if it did. Use your answers to inform your goals and plans for the week ahead. For example, if you noticed that having more frequent breaks actually allowed you to do more work, ask why that is and see how you can keep that going . . . could you optimize by taking even more breaks? Get curious. Make a goal to test your hypotheses.

Step 3: Prioritize

Look at your goas and be realistic about the time, energy, or money you need to achieve them. Rank them according to your main values; for example, identify the key task for everyday that needs to be tackled first in the morning. Delegate where possible, or eliminate those things that are on second thoughts not so important. As you plan your week ahead, you want to include enough time for rest, reflection, and planning. Don't skimp on these things!

Step 4: Adjust

Nothing is set in stone. Good plans and systems are flexible. After all, the whole point is to be constantly fine tuning and adjusting. You don't have to continue with anything that is no longer working. Observe, adjust, try again, and repeat. Incremental improvement is always better than knocking it out of the park on the first try!

Remember, you are focusing on two main points: *why* and *when*. As long as you understand why you are doing a certain task and when, you will feel more organized and focused. Here's an example. Let's say you're a compulsive email checker, so you design a better system. You allocate special times every morning and evening where you make a habit of checking emails. You plan this in your schedule so that you have fewer distractions and can prioritize more "deep work" (already, you have answered the why and when questions).

You might install an app that discourages you from checking emails during certain periods in the day. If you use make time to strategize every Sunday, you might check in and ask how well the app is really working. Maybe you notice it's superfluous; in that case, you delete the app. Your system can be as small as this or ultra-large, encapsulating many sub-systems. But whatever you design, make sure you do it consciously and keep adjusting according to what actually works for you.

Develop a Routine

A routine can be thought of as a choreographed collection of smaller habits, each one flowing into the other effortlessly. Again, routine and habit save the day by reducing your cognitive load and making the *right* thing the *easiest* thing, i.e., making the best decision automatic. Routines are like the foundation of life. Rather than stifling your creativity, they support and allow it—once the nuts and bolts are taken care of, you are free to expand, solve problems, connect, create.

The irony is that those who avoid taking care of daily routines are often the most bogged down with those boring day to day chores and tasks. But a routine makes things easy and simple and gives you a self-esteem boost and the feeling that yes, you are a conscious agent in control of your life, driving it in the direction you want it to go!

Here's a big secret that all ultra-successful people know: humble, incremental changes *always* outperform big, flashy quantum leaps.

It's the small actions that make the biggest difference—if they're done consistently, that is.

Once habits are cemented in your brain, they can be incredibly difficult to shift. So, use that to your advantage and make sure you're almost addicted to doing the right thing.

First things first: you need a morning routine. Entrepreneur Jim Rohn said, "Success is a few simple disciplines practiced every day; while failure is simply a few errors in judgment repeated every day." The way you start your day sets the tone for everything else, so start here when building healthy routines.

Firstly, don't follow any formulas—you are looking for the routine that's right *for you*. Start small. Observe how you go, adjust, try again, observe again. Go slow and don't be afraid to change things up. You might currently wake up at 10:00 each morning but want to do better, for example. The best way is with baby steps— for a week, get up at 9:30, then for another week, make it 9:00, and so on. Don't ask yourself what the biggest change is that you can make, but what the smallest, *most sustainable* change is. What can you easily imagine yourself doing for the next week? Do that. Then ramp up the challenge. Consistency wins out every time.

Other small changes you can make that add up to big results:

- Keep the same wake time and sleep time every day, no matter what

- Make a rule about screen time before bed and after you wake up—perhaps build in an hour window on either side where you stay away from screens

- Do one thing for each of the four main areas of our complete being: **physical, mental, emotional, and spiritual**. Keep balanced by addressing each area every morning; for example, have a healthy breakfast and stretch, set your goals for the day, say a few affirmations, and then finish with a prayer or meditation.

- Start the morning with deep breathing, yoga or stretching, or a walk outside to boot up your system.

- Plan ahead and make a schedule, but be flexible and build in time for the unexpected. You don't have to be your own slave master—if something isn't working, don't give up, just ask what adjustments you can make to move forward.

- Try laying your clothes out the night before, plan your breakfast the night before, and give yourself extra time so you're not rushing.

- Journal, doodle, pray, meditate, or write in a gratitude journal to remind yourself of what really matters to you and why you're making positive changes in the first place. Renew your motivation and commitment.

You'll find plenty of advice out there on the best routines (bullet journaling, sleep hygiene, better organization, etc.), but the key to a good routine is astonishingly simple: pick one positive action and do it today. Then do it again tomorrow. And keep going. That's it. The smaller and humbler, the better. You can try it right now:

1. What is one area you know needs some attention? For example, sleep, nutrition, or organization.

2. What *small, single, repeatable action can* you easily manage to do today? Do it right now. Then do it tomorrow. Repeat until this small action is second nature.

Congratulations, you've achieved what is simultaneously the easiest and yet the hardest part of personal development!

Use Decision Trees

A decision tree is a flow chart style tool you can use to help clarify the decision-making process. Often, procrastination and lack of productivity come down to dawdling on big decisions and being indecisive when concrete action is called for. In a decision tree, you lay out a diagram that shows how one decision can lead to various potential outcomes, with further branches for each subsequent decision. This is an organized, practical way of coming to grips with your options and possibilities and helping you predict consequences so you can make the best choice possible. Often, procrastination problems are a result of anxiety, decision fatigue, or the rumination that comes with endlessly turning over dilemmas in your head without coming to any resolution. A decision tree is a way to stay in control and stay organized.

How do you make a decision tree?

First, sit down with a pen and paper and try to formalize the decision you're facing. For example, you might need to choose between dropping a complicated project or pushing on with it. On the left draw your decision point and then indicate the two branching chains from that point. What happens if you drop the project? Note down all the possible outcomes and then consider which of *those* you'll choose. Note the outcomes again and continue down the chain as far as possible, branching off your decision points and possible outcomes.

Now, a few points: of course it's not possible to literally predict the future. Decision trees are always updated with time, but you are simply acting according to the information you have right now. Once you've made the tree, you obviously have to consider each outcome and choose between them. Most big life problems are complex, however, and you may need to carefully weigh up several features of each choice:

- Consider the risks and costs associated with each action
- Consider the probability or likelihood of an outcome occurring
- Consider opportunity cost (what is lost in taking too long to decide) and the time cost for each decision or outcome
- Consider you bigger goals, your values and principles, and what's ultimately most important to you when making your final decision

On drawing up your tree and considering all the variables at play, you might decide to drop the project since all predicted potential outcomes will not outweigh what you can predict as the costs and risks involved. Look at each outcome and weigh them up against one another, bearing in mind that there will always be the possibility of unexpected outcomes, too. Taking the time to lay it all out clearly, step by step, can bring clarity and focus.

Decision trees are often used in business contexts, and it's worth noting that they aren't always appropriate. They work best when you are quite clear on the life "rules" that will guide a decision and where the choices are few and clearly delineated. They work less well when you lack insight into the options available, or when you don't trust yourself to properly formulate the risks, probabilities and choices available to you.

As a tool to combat procrastination, decision trees can help by getting you organized and focused. The decision might still be hard, but at least you can gain clarity on what's at stake, and what your options are. This pushes you to take informed action sooner, which means you waste less time and energy on useless rumination. The great thing about a decision tree is that is can be updated to reflect each decision and outcome. As you make a choice, new options open up. Amend your tree as you go. Even if you find that decision trees are too complex for you, you might find benefit in training yourself to think beyond the mere decision in front of you. Also ask what future possibilities each choice opens for you and how you'll respond to those. Simply taking this perspective can bring new insight and bring you out worry mode and into action mode.

Understand Interruption Science

Interruption science is the study of human performance, including a myriad of factors affecting productivity. In a modern world filled with push notifications, twenty-four-seven email access and pop-up ads, undivided attention is increasingly a scarce commodity. But understanding how the brain deals with interruptions can help you deal with them effectively and get back to your focused flow of work as quickly as possible.

Interruption science provides insight into why multitasking is so ineffective. Although people believe they are simultaneously performing multiple tasks, they're actually merely *switching* from one task to another in an activity called rapid toggling. Each time an individual changes tasks, it is an interruption. Those interruptions can reduce productivity by as much as forty percent for the typical multitasker and cause an effective ten-point drop in IQ. So, the feeling that you're getting more done is just an illusion!

First things first, don't deliberately interrupt yourself. Set your own timers or limits on internet or social media use and have clearly defined periods where you check mail, etc. It's all about pre-emptively controlling your exposure to things that might derail your work. Next, avoid "busy work" that is really unnecessary. It's better to begin each day with your largest, most important task first instead of the false sense of productivity you get from ticking many tiny tasks off the list. Go through your to-do list and rank tasks in order, deliberately avoiding tackling the unimportant ones until the more urgent ones are done.

If you are interrupted, no problem. Make a quick note of the message/request/whatever and power on, telling yourself you'll explore it later at an appropriate time (provided it's not a massive emergency). Another great way to minimize distractions is to batch your tasks so that you're doing similar activities together and minimizing time spent switching. Do all your computer work in one go, get all your errands done on one car trip, or block all your meetings together so you're doing all your discussing and brainstorming at one time. Having a clear schedule with a non-negotiable booking of what you'll be doing in each block will help you delegate tasks, shelf them for later, or even simply ignore them.

For maximum effectiveness, you want to create a steady, uninterrupted workflow state that is as simple as possible, rather than having a fractured, chaotic, and complex day made up of millions of different tasks. The latter usually just makes you *feel* busy but in fact reduces your overall efficacy.

It's a good idea to set up a deliberate email and communications policy, rather than just fielding every message and email that comes in no matter what. Dedicate a set amount of time at set points in the day to do emails, and forget about it outside of this window—especially early in the morning or late at night!

Reducing interruptions and distractions in your work may mean setting non-negotiable boundaries with colleagues or family so they know when you're busy and for how long and will not disrupt you. You might decide to have a "closed door means leave me alone" policy or put a little sign on your desk to show that you're in work mode and not to be disturbed. Set up your office to minimize distractions or move to an entirely different spot where you can have more privacy. Make liberal use of timers and alarms to block off periods of time—say twenty-five minutes—where you hunker down and work on that task and nothing else. Noise-cancelling headphones work wonders; they make it harder for people to come and talk to you while you're busy and they also block out random noise from the environment.

Takeaways:

- Productivity is a consistent habit and not a single action. Fortunately, a few healthy habits can build the foundation for a lifetime of focus and effectiveness.
- One way to make sure that inevitable distractions are not derailing your work and focus is to keep a distraction list. As you work and a distraction pops up, write it in a notebook and simply carry on, putting it out of your mind. You can take action on the noted items later, when and if *you* choose to. Convert those worries into actionable tasks and set a time when you'll do them.
- Consistently act to reduce the overall cognitive load by giving yourself fewer decisions to make. This will stop you getting overwhelmed with decision fatigue or paralyzed in indecision. Get firm on your priorities, delegate when necessary, and be firm in ignoring things that truly don't matter. Automate as much

as possible by using "life rules" and habit rather than making decisions afresh each time. Stick with tried and true options so you're not reinventing the wheel with every decision.

- A system is an organized collection of rules, values, principles, priorities, and limits that reduces the mental bandwidth needed whilst ensuring you're doing the optimal thing at all times. Focusing on the *why* and *when* of your actions, take time at regular intervals to contemplate, make a plan, do it, appraise your results, and adjust accordingly. Sunday evenings are a great time to appraise the past week and plan the week ahead.

- Make sure you are consciously choosing effective daily routines that address all four areas of your being: physical, emotional, mental, and spiritual. Healthy morning routines are essential.

- For complex decisions, use decision trees to help you stay organized and focused on what matters. Clearly identify your choice points, their probable outcomes, and what choices you'll make in response to those outcomes. Choose the best outcome, bearing in mind the role of the unexpected in mind. Note also that not every decision is suited to a decision tree analysis.

- Do what you can to avoid, minimize, and quickly recover from life's inevitable interruptions. Don't multitask. Work in longer blocks of time or batches, set boundaries, and avoid distractions. Do your most important task first, when you're most alert. If you are interrupted, use the distraction list to soother your anxious brain and tell it, "You don't need to keep reminding me, I will remember this. Just not now."

Chapter 9: Tips for Mastering the Psychology of Motivation

"Knowing others is intelligence; knowing yourself is true wisdom. Mastering others is strength; mastering yourself is true power."

- Lao Tzu

Identify Your Work Patterns

Tracking your time, even if no one is asking you to do it, can help you understand your work habits and the time of day when you finish work most successfully. This might hold the key to being more productive because learning from your patterns will allow you to focus on where you are (and aren't) most productive.

Every one of us has a peak period of productivity—maximizing your efficiency is often just a question of scheduling your most important or difficult work during this period. Knowledge is power—that is, *self*-knowledge is power!

What are your tech habits and how do they affect your process?
Where do you lose/waste time during the day? Doing what and when?
When is your peak productivity time and when are you least enthusiastic and focused?
What are your social media, email, and web-browsing habits like?
Are you a morning/night person?
When are your riskiest times of day for procrastination and distraction?
How is your innate "body clock" interacting with your work obligations?
How long can you typically work on something before needing a rest?
What's easy for you and what is more difficult task-wise?
What usually energizes you most?

Understanding exactly what is going on is the first step to making meaningful adjustments. Data is extremely useful. The previous tip emphasized the importance of reviewing your progress and adjusting accordingly—data about what you're actually doing day to day will help you achieve this faster than hunches or guesses or assumptions.

One way to start gathering data on your existing habits and strengths is to take one full week where you simply observe yourself in action. Keep a simple diary where you note your:

- Energy levels
- Ability to focus and concentrate
- Creativity and natural problem-solving ability

Time management and discipline mean nothing if you're only using them to force yourself into a routine that goes against your natural flow. Once you've had the chance to notice your daily and weekly rhythms, then you can step in a schedule work for your strongest periods and rest for your lowest-energy periods (remembering to adjust as you go—there is some trial and error involved).

Finally, once you've gotten to understand yourself a bit better, see if you can identify and work with your unique work style. Everyone has their own productivity peaks and troughs, but your work style is more about *how* you go about your work every day.

Independent

You work best alone, under your own steam and direction. You are productive, efficient, and disciplined, especially when left to follow your own vision. *Maximize your efficiency by gaining as much autonomy as possible, or even seek out entrepreneurship.*

Cooperative

You function best in a group and are an excellent communicator and diplomat. You love when a project emerges via mutual collaboration. *Maximize your efficiency by carefully choosing the team you work with, and select those who will appreciate and make use of your input.*

Proximity

A mix between the two above. You work best with others but like to maintain some independent responsibility. Your strength is versatility and you can adapt to different modes as needed. *Maximize your efficiency by asking where you need more independence and where you need more cooperation.*

Supportive

You get to the emotional core of any project. You are a natural facilitator and cheerleader, and celebrate the success of the group effort. *Maximize your efficiency by choosing projects and colleagues that "get" your skill set and will acknowledge and reward it.*

Guardian or timekeeper

Detail-oriented and focused on order and organization, you act as the workplace's conscience. You are risk-averse, pragmatic, and stable. *Maximize your efficiency by partnering with other work types who you can trust to inspire, lead, and support you.*

Big picture

You understand the broader vision and can think in theories and models, integrating ideas, and identifying overall patterns. You're excellent at predicting outcomes as well as trouble shooting. *Maximize your efficiency by getting out of theory mode and into active leadership—can you take on more responsibility somewhere?*

As you can see, when it comes to productivity and success, there is no one size fits all. Whichever way you choose to slice it, constantly ask yourself in the back of your mind: who am I? How do I work? And how can I arrange my external environment to best support what I am already naturally doing?

Take More Breaks

Let's stay with this idea that your mental resources are finite and get depleted over time. Your mind is not some free-floating abstract thing—it's your brain, which is a physical organ, which runs on glucose and gets tired just as surely as anything else in your body can get tired. In the ongoing quest for better productivity, we can lose sight of the fact that our bodies have physiological limits. But rest is not optional. It's key to recharging and refreshing our brains so that we can learn, process, evolve . . . and achieve greater efficiency moving forward.

First things first: taking breaks does not mean you're lazy. Taking a break isn't a sign of giving up or an admission that the work is too difficult. A break is not something you "earn" by working too hard. And finally, a break is not a luxury that you build in when you have time. Have you ever skipped breaks because you wanted to get more done? The truth is you probably got less done.

Increasingly, the research is showing that breaks are a big part of staying productive. Without breaks, decision fatigue builds, your concentration and focus diminish as the glucose in your brain runs out, your eyes become strained, and your mood may even dip. But resting your brain gives it time to absorb, process, and consolidate what's been learned, refresh itself, and return to work with better memory, more energy, creativity, and focus.

Not all breaks are created equal, however. Opinions vary slightly, but the consensus seems to be that:
- The ideal frequency is once every fifty to ninety minutes—this depends on the type of work. More difficult, new, or strenuous work is best done in shorter

chunks. Observe your own fatigue signals and adjust accordingly.

- The ideal break length is around five to fifteen minutes. Every two to four hours, take a longer break—say for around thirty minutes.

- Good activities to do on your break are obviously anything unrelated to work. It's a good idea to avoid the internet or screens in general, and try to get up and move, stretch, breathe. A walk is a perfect stress buster, too, as is a friendly chat or just a quiet moment of resting or meditating.

- Naps during a break can work, provided you don't find they make you groggy or interfere with your regular sleep routine. You don't need to fall fully asleep to feel refreshed—dozing a little somewhere dark and quiet is also good.

- Have a small, healthy snack to replenish your brain glucose, or enjoy a cup of coffee (if it's not too late in the day and you're not overly sensitive to caffeine).

- Take a moment to doodle, daydream, or tinker with a hobby. The idea is to completely disengage your work brain and allow it to recuperate.

- If taking a break genuinely is impossible, then you may find some relief in simply switching task or tackling a different aspect of the task or working on it in a different way. In the long term, however, you may need to make some longer term lifestyle changes so that you're never forced to go without proper breaks during the day.

Breaks are important. Don't wait until you're completely tapped out and grumpy to take a break—schedule them in deliberately on your calendar, or set an alarm or reminder, and follow through. I know it can be incredibly difficult to carve out time for a break, especially when you're surrounded by workaholics or colleagues who don't understand. It might help to agree well ahead of time the breaks you'll be taking and why, so they know what to expect. Then, defend that time!

While you're having a break, take the time to be mindful of what you're doing and why—it's not "nothing." Spare a thought for how much your brain really does for you and be grateful for your cognitive faculties. Focus on how good it feels to rest and recuperate, and zoom in on all the benefits you're accruing by taking a break. This will reinforce the break habit in your life. Soon, you'll be cherishing your break time and relishing the renewed focus and enthusiasm it gives you to do the things you want to.

Reward Yourself

Yes, achieving your goal is a reward in itself. But the truth is that actively acknowledging and marking your milestones is a necessary part of ongoing success. Knowing *how* to reward yourself matters too. If you reach a goal, celebrate with something that won't set you back. After all, it doesn't make sense to reward yourself by undoing all your hard work and sending your unconscious mind a self-defeating message. A reward should not be an excuse for harmful indulgence. And they should never be your *only* reason for doing something. You want your rewards to leave you feeling validated, cared for, strengthened, and excited to carry on with your mission.

Dopamine is the brain's reward neurotransmitter. It tells your body, "This is good, keep on doing this!" If you use appropriate rewards, you build positive associations with healthy behaviors, reinforcing your commitment. On the other hand, making any task feel like a punishment can backfire—when you don't feel good, you're far more likely to give up or get bored.

It's about using positive reinforcement to build momentum. Especially for bigger goals, you need to regularly stop and see how far you've come. You need to feel like you're making progress, or else you'll lose interest and motivation—nobody wants to slog away at something without feeling like they are getting somewhere with it or doing a good job. Give yourself that feedback.

How? First, match the size of the achievement to the size of the reward. For example, if you've just completed a grueling four-hour exam, take the afternoon off and go on an hour long walk in your favorite location, get a manicure, or treat yourself to a meal at that restaurant you love. As you're enjoying your reward, really take the time to pause and relish it. Tell yourself—out loud if possible—that you've come far, you're doing great, and you deserve a nice treat. You want to literally feel the pleasure and reward in your brain and connect that to the achievement you've just made. This is to reinforce that dopamine reward system. Give yourself a pat on the back and internalize the feeling that you are improving, and you're going to keep going because *it feels good*.

Don't be tempted to choose a reward you think you should want—just go into kid mode and choose something completely irrational and fun, just for the sake of it! Likewise, don't allow yourself to feel guilty for taking a rest from working. Remember that rewards are a little like save points in video games. Think of the boost of dopamine as a way to bank and consolidate your progress so far and affirm to yourself and others that you are on the right track. The encouragement will in fact inspire you to keep going even further.

Here's a simple way to understand the reward process:

1. Design a trigger for yourself to cue the desired behavior—for example, an alarm that wakes you up in the morning.
2. Go through the behavior, in this case actually waking up on time.
3. Reward yourself as soon as possible in recognition of the desired behavior. Let's say you allow yourself to have a fancier frothy coffee in the morning if you wake up on time.
4. Enjoy your special coffee and take a quick moment to think to yourself, *Mm, yum, delicious coffee. Waking up early is great.*

You can set up tiny, regular rewards for yourself as in the above example. They act as constant reinforcers. Or, you could have larger and more intermittent rewards on the way to bigger goals. For example, if you're training for a marathon, you could celebrate your first 5k run, then celebrate every additional kilometer after that, and so on. Just make sure that your rewards are a) in proportion to your achievements, b) actually meaningful to you, i.e., they feel good to you personally and have no other replacement, and c) don't cancel your achievement.

Here's a quick way to start using rewards to break through productivity barriers: write down three tasks that you're procrastinating. Then decide on an appropriate reward for completing each one. If you complete the task, enjoy your reward and notice how you feel—isn't it amazing what achievement and reward do for your self-esteem?

Be Prepared for Resistance

There's no way around it: at some point on your journey, you **will** be tempted to quit.

The best way to make sure you power through that impulse is to be prepared and make a plan well *before* you find yourself with depleted motivation and unable to fight cravings. We all have urges to give up, but they are mostly unconscious. One of the most powerful things you can do to improve your productivity and effectiveness is to be more conscious of those urges. A good exercise is to go through the day with a bit of paper and put a tally mark each time you get an urge. For example, every time you want to skip gym, waste time online, or guzzle tubs of ice cream. At first, simply become aware of the urges and when they happen.

Once you do this, you're in a position to make an informed plan to tackle those urges when (not if) they emerge. Write this plan down, too.

By identifying triggers that cause your resolve to waver, you can pre-empt them and manage them before they overwhelm you. The classic example is to never go shopping on an empty stomach or when you're stressed or sad, especially if you know that this state of mind triggers you to buy unhealthy foods. Similarly, if you know that you are always tempted to check your phone in the morning and this can easily set off a procrastination cycle that you later regret, nip it in the bud by putting your phone in another room overnight and only allowing yourself to check it after you've completed your morning routine as normal.

Having slip-ups or difficult moments is inevitable, but you can take control by pre-empting those moments and having a rock solid plan to fall back on. A great idea is to build in this plan while you're making goals and deadlines for yourself. For example, you might be assigned a project at university that's due in three weeks. Make your plan for how you'll tackle the problem, but simultaneously make a plan for the things you already know will jeopardize that plan. So, you might deliberately schedule work on the project in the morning when you're most alert, install a desktop app to limit your internet browsing, or have a word with friends and family to ask them not to invite you out or distract you in that final week before the deadline.

How do you know what fail safes to build into your plan? Again, it comes down to self-knowledge. If you've failed in the past, ask yourself why. Become curious about what you can do to prevent the same from happening in future. Be realistic as you look and appraise the potential risk zones and put extra support in place. How you do this will depend on the goal you're trying to achieve as well as your unique weaknesses and predispositions. But here are a few helpful ways to pull yourself through temptations to quit:

Avoid any triggers or stimuli entirely. Don't rely on your willpower alone to valiantly fight off temptation—just don't be near it in the first place.

Replace anything that threatens your progress with something better. For example, if you're trying to quit smoking, take up chewing gum, or do something else on your "smoke breaks" at work.

Remind yourself of your commitment. Before falling off the wagon, dig deep and recall all those big dreams you want to achieve, your values, your hopes. In the face of defeat is where your resolve is truly tested—if you can push through, you'll feel so much better about yourself and be better prepared next time.

Distract yourself. Cravings and temptations are often fleeting. As much as possible, forcefully remove your attention from the temptation and wait out the urge.

Get support from others, whether that's in a formal support group, from a mentor, or from simply sharing your dreams and fears with friends and family. If you feel yourself wavering, reach out and ask for help.

Stay healthy. Often, our willpower is weakest when we are under slept, poorly nourished, stressed, or unhappy. Give yourself the best chance of sticking to resolutions by taking care of your physical health as much as possible.

Finally, **practice forgiveness**. It's not the end of the world to slip up. In fact, as soon as can, accept it, learn what you can from the mistake, and immediately take action in the right direction. Don't dwell on it—you'll only discourage yourself and feel bad. The best thing to do with a slip-up is to process it into a lesson and use it to power you further on your path. Beating yourself up about (inevitable) setbacks does exactly nothing to get you closer to your goal! Positive action is the only thing that gets you there. So, focus on that.

Learn to Say NO to Things that Don't Add Value

Remember, productivity is not just doing the thing right; it is also about doing the right thing. Staying focused and productive is as much about what you *do* as what you *don't do*. That's why it's super important to say no to any work that does not align with your goals and mission—think of it as saying yes to what does align.

It's not easy to say no, but it's the only way to focus on work that matters. Are you one of those people who says yes when they mean no? It's important to know why you do this. Usually, weak boundaries and people-pleasing comes from a strong desire to be liked, or a misplaced belief that we are ultimately responsible for the happiness and wellbeing of others. Once we address this core belief, we are in a better position to set up healthy boundaries according to our values. A carefully crafted no can enable both parties to engage in a more productive discussion and align on the outcomes.

Sounds good in theory, but here's how to practice putting your foot down in everyday life.

Step 1: Get right with yourself first

Your no needs to come from a place of genuine clarity and conviction. You need to know fully in yourself *why* you are saying no, and really believe in your right and freedom to do so. Sort this out for yourself and your no will be taken seriously. Whether you're setting up a small boundary or a big one, prepare yourself first. Think about what you'll say and how you'll say it. Remember, you are not setting restrictions or conditions on other people's behavior, but your own. Do what you need to to let go of the fear of their reaction—that's simply not your business. Keep grounded by continually asking, what are you trying to achieve and what is your goal? What are you responsible for and what is the other person responsible for?

Step 2: Pay attention to your technique

If you're a big softie and a pushover, saying no will take practice at first. When you are communicating a boundary to someone, it's best to stay polite but keep it simple. Don't elaborate, don't apologize, and don't "hedge," i.e., overexplain, ask permission, or try to soften what you're saying. Keep short and sweet and *don't budge.* If people push on that limit, simply reaffirm it politely, as many times as you need to. Be assertive, honor your own needs, and notice that you can say no to others without being responsible for their reactions. Try some of these phrases, said simply and politely:

Thanks for thinking of me, but I have too much on my plate right now.

Not for me, thanks.

I'm afraid I can't.

I'm not really into [whatever], but thanks for asking!

I think I'll pass.

Step 3: Follow through

Having good boundaries is a habit. Once you assert your needs, follow through and keep following through. If you've said no and someone disrespects that, follow up with consequences. Be ruthless with those who do not take your limits and preferences seriously. Do not bend over backward to accommodate those who don't reciprocate your consideration. Walk away from situations where your boundaries are continually disrespected, but at the same time notice when saying no actually gets you what you want. You may need to practice getting over your initial awkwardness, but you also may be surprised at just how readily people will respect your boundaries when you respect them first yourself.

Of course, life can get complicated and it can be a challenge to put your foot down sometimes. It may be necessary occasionally to simply buy time ("Can I get back to you on that?") or make a white lie/excuse ("I'm sorry, I can't be there. I already made plans"). Whatever you do, keep things short and sweet. You don't have to follow up your no with any consolation or apology. Remember, it's your responsibility to manage your own emotions, resources, time, and expectations, and it's other people's responsibility to manage theirs.

Often people say yes when they should say no because they want to appear useful or likeable, they don't want to offend, or they feel they have no choice. But this is an illusion, since being a "doormat" often only leads to resentment later on, since people typically have less respect for you, not more.

Trust your gut, be assertive, and keep consistent—it does get easier!

Takeaways:

- Mastering the psychology of productivity and focus requires a deep degree of self-knowledge and knowing how to work with your own inbuilt strengths, weaknesses, and preferences.

- Identify your own workflow throughout the day and find the hours you're most energized, creative and alert so you can schedule the day's most important tasks for then.

- Consider also what your unique work style is and how you can support this to get the most from your time. You could be more independent, cooperative, a mix of both ("proximity"), supportive, a big-picture thinker, or a guardian/timekeeper. Your preferred style of work will typically be your most effortlessly productive, so try to identify your style and then make adjustments so you are supporting yourself.

- Appropriate breaks are nonnegotiable and allow the brain to rest, recuperate, and consolidate the work it has done. Energy and focus are finite resources and need to be replenished. Take a break for five to fifteen minutes every fifty to ninety minutes, with a longer break every two to four hours. Take a power nap, go for a walk, stretch, meditate, have a snack or drink, or even just switch tasks.

- Dopamine is the brain's reward chemical and signals "this is good, do it again." Make use of positive reinforcement by rewarding desired behavior to make it more likely to be repeated in the future. Choose rewards that are proportionate to your achievement, meaningful, and which don't undermine the progress you've made. Focus on the pleasure and feeling of accomplishment to drive home the reward and encourage more forward momentum.

- Resistance, slip-ups, and setbacks are inevitable. Be prepared. Without judgment, identify the triggers that cause you to give up, and then act in future to avoid them or replace them with something else. Ask for help, distract yourself until the craving passes, or take a moment to remind yourself of your deepest commitment and values. Most importantly, forgive yourself if you slip up and take action on the right path as soon as possible.

- Finally, set good boundaries and say no to whatever is not helping your ultimate mission. Before saying no, prepare yourself and find clarity and conviction, then take an approach that is simple, polite, and firm. Repeat if necessary. Follow through and keep practicing. It will get easier with time!